Prayers at 3 A.M.

Prayers at 3 A.M.

Poems, Songs, Chants, and
Prayers for the Middle of the Night

Edited by Phil Cousineau

HarperSanFrancisco
A Division of HarperCollins*Publishers*

Permissions appear on page 231.

PRAYERS AT 3 A.M. *Poems, Songs, Chants, and Prayers for the Middle of the Night.*
Copyright © 1995 by Phil Cousineau. All rights reserved. Printed in the United
States of America. No part of this book may be used or reproduced in any manner
whatsoever without written permission except in the case of brief quotations
embodied in critical articles and reviews. For information address HarperCollins
Publishers, 10 East 53rd Street, New York, NY 10022.

FIRST EDITION
Book design by Ralph Fowler
Set in Stempel Schneidler by TBH Typecast

Library of Congress Cataloging-in-Publication Data
Prayers at 3 a.m. : poems, songs, chants, and prayers
for the middle of the night / edited by Phil Cousineau.
—1st ed.
p.   cm.
ISBN 0–06–2501200–5 (cloth: alk. paper)
1. Night—Literary collections.   I. Cousineau, Phil.
PN6071.N5P73   1995   94–38900
808.8'033—dc20   CIP

95 96 97 98 99 HAD 10 9 8 7 6 5 4 3 2 1

This edition is printed on acid-free paper that meets the American National
Standards Institute Z39.48 Standard.

Contents

Burning the Midnight Oil, 101

The Dark Night of the Soul, 131

Reconciling with the Night, 163

To my sister,
Nicole Marie Cousineau-Black

I have read three hours, then: mine eyes are weak:
Fold down the leaf where I have left: to bed:
Take not away the taper, leave it burning;
And if thou canst awake by four o' the clock,
I prithee, call me. Sleep hath seized me wholly.

"Cymbeline," William Shakespeare

Every man prays in his own language,
and there is no language that
God does not understand.

Duke Ellington, Grace Cathedral, 1965

Prayer is better than sleep.

Isabelle Eberhardt

Preface

Night, the dark bridge across the chasm of our days, can be an exhila-
rating or anxious crossing. Whether watching the sun set, slumbering in
bed, burning the midnight oil, squirming from insomnia, howling from
full-moon lunacy, praying for divine guidance, or dreaming of Gothic
castles, we slip across the hours of darkness as if into another world.

Throughout the centuries, attempts to fathom the dark blue mys-
teries of the night have been rendered in myths, legends, poems,
songs, lullabies, riddles, hymns, and prayers. Their alternately com-
forting and combustible words and images reflect the bittersweet ride
many people have on the nightly journey from dusk till dawn.

Out of the ancient desire to "eat the darkness," as old world fabu-
lators describe the power of firelight storytelling, emerges my own
collection of night owl reflections, *Prayers at 3 A.M.* As an anthology for
all those who are fascinated by the world after dark, it eulogizes the
proverbial idea that "prayer is night descended upon thought."

For me, the compilation is a contemporary *noctuary,* a journal of
nocturnal contemplations that aspires to be a source of inspiration for
the nighthawk at the all-night diner, an insomniac's guide to the dark

night of the soul, or a beguiling companion book to sit alongside the warm brandy on the bedstand. It also embraces the paradox implicit in a book for those who find themselves up in the middle of the night, since it seems half the world reads to wake up, the other half to go to sleep.

The convergence is in the ancient idea of prayer itself. For Homer, the reason for prayer was that "all men need the aid of the gods." To Muslims, prayer is a ladder, a journey reaching to heaven. St. Thérèse of Lisieux called it "an uplifting of the heart." In the words of William James, prayer is "the soul and essence of religion," and to Auguste Sabatier, "religion in action." According to the Dakota Sioux physician and author, Ohiyesa, "In the life of the Indian there was only one inevitable duty,—the duty of prayer—the daily recognition of the Unseen and Eternal." Mahatma Gandhi practiced a "prayer that needs no speech," and Thomas Merton struggled for a form of prayer in everyday life "with everything I touch." For Brother David Steindl-Rast, "Prayer is unlimited mindfulness."

Together, these night thoughts vividly illustrate Alfred North Whitehead's liberating description of religion as *what we do with our solitude.*

Prayers at 3 A.M. combines the traditional idea of prayer as inner dialogue with God with the tribal belief that daily devotion blesses the sacredness of life. It links them both to a wide range of poetic contemplations on the profound depths of the human struggle with the inscrutable night. Here is where the line between prayer and poetry blurs. The selections for the phantasmagorical hours between sleep and waking can then be evocative of Henry David Thoreau's river reverie, where "Our truest life is when we are in dreams awake."

The nightwriters on this vesperal road range from saints, poets, and shamans to monks, astronomers, naturalists, and the anonymous authors of ancient tales. Among them they ponder the falling darkness, revel in dreamtime, convey the ache of melancholy, concoct recipes against sleeplessness, vanquish the loneliness of hotel rooms, contemplate the night sky, rhapsodize on love, and languorously greet the first rays of dawn. They are lovers of the dark way, moving instinctively through the cloud of unknowing, the unexplored wood. Again and again, these rhapsodies on the theme point back and down to, as all soulful language does, the root word: *prayer* from *precarius,* which meant "to entreat, implore, ask," but also "to request, to look again, seek out."

So out of the vast night descends a "precarious" power over our souls that inspires us to ask our most vital questions and challenges us to look within and seek without. For night is the time, as Pawnee Indians sing, when "visions travel better." The hour Benedictine monks believe the world need prayers more than ever. The moment Buddhist monks experience the lowest flame of Kundalini. The dark night of the soul. The dark wall. The midpoint of our nightly soul journey. The black ink from God's pen.

When we're sitting quietly with the great mysteries, doing nothing, the soul deepens, prayers happen all by themselves. Some of the words that emerge out of those meditations are meant to rouse us, others to send us into sweet slumber. *Which are which?*

Listening to these night voices, we become alert to a world rapidly disappearing under the artificial light of the modern world. Despite our predatory fears, the night is long and full of marvels. By the light of its dark secrets we can make our own way through the shadowworld to the fire at the source of all mystery.

Phil Cousineau
San Francisco
September 1994

The Rush of Darkness

From Chaos and Darkness, the Greeks believed, came black-winged Night, the mother of doom, old age, and death, but also sleep, dream, friendship, the Three Fates, and Eros, the desirable. More than just the absence of day, the dark that brings on night is a presence in itself, a shadowplay of mythic force.

The nocturnal voices in this opening section remind us that night is more than earth's dark turn away from the sun. A mystery is suddenly upon us. Day seems nothing but a nightbound train. Light disappears. Darkness rushes in. Swiftly, night comes on. "There had been a rhythm of the day and now there was a rhythm of the night," as Padraic Colum once portrayed the twilight arrival of the Irish storyteller.

For the Shintos of Japan, sunset is the moment to speak reverently in the presence of the Great Parent God. For Rumi, the Sufi ecstatic, when "the sun slides down" a "route to the invisible opens." William Blake, in his "Night" reverie, describes the curious venturing out of the soul at dusk:

> The sun descending in the west,
> The evening star does shine
> The birds are silent in their nest,
> And I must seek for mine.

What is it that the poet seeks? What does he or she ask of the night? What is pressing about the tumbling darkness? Clearly, there are dark secrets.

The night writers at the rush of darkness urgently seek the thread of silence that stills the souls of birds and humans alike. What once was known as a "call to prayer" from church bells or minarets is now for many a secularized hue and cry for attention to the life of the here and now. "Caress the details, the divine details," once wrote Vladimir Nabokov. The voices here tell us that there is a fire in the night that must be tended, as in the legend of Baal Shem-Tov—prayers to be learned then handed down, the very meaning of tradition. They suggest that although words may not save our souls, they can help us turn our attention around so "our eyes look inward," in the words of the nineteenth-century Persian poet Ghalib. The Romantic poet Novalis reveals the source of his inspiration in one of his "Hymns to the Night," his "unchangeable, eternal faith in the heaven of Night." In "Summer Night," by Joy Harjo, the poet writes of "the secret / of your own flower of light / blooming in the miraculous dark." For philosopher James P. Carse, an experience of the sacred in ordinary life will not come easily in these harried days; we need ritualized time more than ever to hear the world of "night speakers . . . declaring their thousand knowledges." William Stafford, in his poem "Listening," recalls his father's remarkable attentiveness to the "soft wild night" and how the family learned to wait for the time when that "something in the night / will touch us too from that other place."

Since at least the ancient Celtic mysteries, dusk has been considered the symbolic time where the two ever-changing worlds meet. The flux between light and dark marks the time of transfiguration. In "Baruch Spinoza," Jorge Luis Borges has a vision in his labyrinthine imagination of the philosopher "building God in the twilight." Standing in the crepuscular hour, Thomas Hardy, in his majestic poem "Afterwards," wonders if others, while watching "the full-starred heavens" after he's gone, will remember him as one "who had an eye for such mysteries."

The question hovers. The night moves on, revealing stars and sleep and the darkness that restores.

From Songs of Owl Woman

In the Blue Night

How shall I begin my song
In the blue night that is settling?
I will sit here and begin my song.

In the Dark I Enter

I can not make out what I see.
In the dark I enter.
I can not make out what I see.

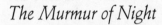

In the Great Night

In the great night my heart will go out,
Toward me the darkness comes rattling,
In the great night my heart will go out.

Owl Woman (Juana Manwell), fl. 1880?
translated from Papago by Frances Densmore

The Murmur of Night

This is the account, here it is:

Now it still ripples, now it still murmurs, ripples, it still
sighs, still hums, and it is empty under the sky.

Here follow the first words, the first eloquence:

There is not yet one person, one animal, bird, fish, crab,
tree, rock, hollow, canyon, meadow, forest. Only the sky
alone is there; the face of the earth is not clear. Only the
sea alone is pooled under all the sky; there is nothing what-
ever gathered together. It is at rest; not a single thing stirs.
It is held back, kept at rest under the sky.

Whatever there is that might be is simply not there: only
the pooled water, only the calm sea, only it alone is pooled.

Whatever might be is simply not there: only murmurs,
ripples, in the dark, in the night. Only the Maker, Modeler

alone, Sovereign Plumed Serpent, the Bearers, Begetters are in the water, a glittering light. They are there, they are enclosed in quetzal feathers, in blue-green.

Thus the name, "Plumed Serpent." They are great knowers, great thinkers in their very being.

And of course there is the sky, and there is also the Heart of Sky. This is the name of the god, as it is spoken.

> *from the Popol Vuh*
> transcribed in Spanish in the 16th century
> translated from modern Quiché Maya by Dennis Tedlock

◑

The Birth of Night

First of all, the Void (*Chaos*) came into being, next broad-bosomed Earth, the solid and eternal home of all, and Eros [Desire], the most beautiful of the immortal gods, who in every man and every god softens the sinews and overpowers the prudent purpose of the mind. Out of Void came Darkness and black Night, and out of Night came Light and Day, her children conceived after union in love with Darkness. Earth first produced starry Sky, equal in size with herself, to cover her on all sides. Next she produced the tall mountains, the pleasant haunts of the gods, and also gave birth to the barren waters, sea with its raging surges—all this without

the passion of love. Thereafter she lay with Sky and gave
birth to Ocean with its deep current.

> *Hesiod*
> from *The Theogony,* 8th century B.C.E.
> translated from ancient Greek by Norman O. Brown

Night Births

At the time when the earth became hot
At the time when the heavens turned about
At the time when the sun was darkened
To cause the moon to shine
The time of the rise of the Pleiades
The slime, this was the source of the earth
The source of the darkness that made darkness
The source of the night that made night
The intense darkness, the deep darkness
Darkness of the sun, darkness of the night
 Nothing but night

> *Hawaiian creation chant,* 20th century
> translated by Martha Warren Beckwith

A Tahitian Family Prayer

This ancient prayer was repeated each night, in former times.

> Save me! Save me! it is the night of the gods. Watch close to me, my God (*atua*)! Close to me, oh, my Lord (*fatu*)! Protect me from enchantments, sudden death, evil conduct, from slandering or being slandered, from intrigue, and from quarrels concerning the limits of land. Let peace reign about us, oh, my God! Protect me from the furious warrior, who spreads terror, whose hair bristles! May I and my spirit live and rest in peace this night, oh my God.

> translated by E. S. Craighill Handy from J. A. Moerenhout

The Girl of the Early Race Who Made the Stars

> My mother was the one who told me that the girl arose; she put her hands into the wood ashes; she threw up the wood ashes into the sky. She said to the wood ashes: "The wood ashes which are here, they must altogether become the Milky Way. They must white lie along in the sky, that the Stars may stand outside of the Milky Way, while the Milky Way is the Milky Way, while it used to be wood ashes." They the ashes altogether become the Milky Way. The Milky Way must go round with the stars; while the Milky

Way feels that, the Milky Way lies going around; while the stars sail along; therefore, the Milky Way, lying, goes along with the Stars. The Milky Way, when the Milky Way stands upon the earth, the Milky Way turns across in front, while the Milky Way means to wait, while the Milky Way feels that the Stars are turning back; while the Stars feel that the Sun is the one who has turned back; he is upon his path; the Stars turn back; while they go to fetch the daybreak; that they may lie nicely, while the Milky Way lies nicely. The Stars shall also stand nicely around. They shall sail along upon their footprints, which they, always sailing along, are following. While they feel that, they are the Stars which descend.

The Milky Way lying comes to its place, to which the girl threw up the wood ashes, that it may descend nicely; it had lying gone along, while it felt that it lay upon the sky. It had lying gone round, while it felt that the Stars also turned round. They turning round passed over the sky. The sky lies still; the Stars are those which go along; while they feel that they sail. They had been setting; they had, again, been coming out; they had, sailing along, been following their footprints. They become white, when the Sun comes out. The Sun sets, they stand around above; while they feel that they did turning follow the Sun.

The darkness comes out; they the Stars wax red, while they had at first been white. They feel that they stand brightly around; that they may sail along; while they feel that it is night. Then, the people go by night; while they feel that the ground is made light. While they feel that the Stars shine a little. Darkness is upon the ground. The Milky Way gently glows; while it feels that it is wood ashes. Therefore, it gently glows. While it feels that the girl was the one who said that the Milky Way should give a little light for the people, that they might return home by night, in the middle of the night. For, the earth would not have been a little light, had not the Milky Way been there. It and the Stars.

‖kábbo
African Bushman, 19th century
translated by Wilhelm H. I. Bleek and Lucy C. Lloyd

And Is It Night?

And is it night? Are they thine eyes that shine?
    Are we alone and here and here alone?
May I come near, may I but touch thy shrine?
    Is Jealousy asleep, and is he gone?
O Gods, no more, silence my lips with thine,
    Lips, kisses, joys, hap, blessings most divine.

O come, my dear, our griefs are turn'd to night,
    And night to joys, night blinds pale Envy's eyes,

Silence and sleep prepare us our delight,
　　O cease we then our woes, our griefs, our cries,
O vanish words, words do but passions move,
　　O dearest life, joys sweet, O sweetest love.

　　　　Anonymous

◐

A Sudanese Evening Prayer

Now that the sun has set,
I sit and rest, and think of you.
Give my weary body peace.
Let my legs and arms stop aching,
Let my nose stop sneezing,
Let my head stop thinking.
Let me sleep in your arms.

　　　traditional Dinka

◐

A Shinto Evening Prayer

I reverently speak in the presence of the Great Parent God:
I give Thee grateful thanks that Thou hast enabled me to live
this day, the whole day, in obedience to the excellent spirit
of Thy ways.

　　　traditional Japanese

from *The Navajo Song of the Earth*

And the night of darkness
And the dawn of light,
    Meeting, joining one another,
    Helpmates ever, they.
        All is beautiful,
        All is beautiful,
        All is beautiful, indeed.

translated by Natalie Curtis Burlin

Evening Prayer

At the time of evening prayer
    everyone spreads cloth and candles,
But I dream of my beloved,
    see, lamenting, grieved, his phantom.
My ablution is with weeping,
    thus my prayer will be fiery,
And I burn the mosque's doorway
    when my call to prayer strikes it. . . .
Is the prayer of the drunken,
    tell me, is this prayer valid?
For he does not know the timing
    and is not aware of places.

Did I pray for two full cycles?
>Or is this perhaps the eighth one?
And which Sura did I utter?
>For I have no tongue to speak it.
At God's door—how could I knock now,
>For I have no hand or heart now?
You have carried heart and hand, God!
>Grant me safety, God, forgive me. . . .

>*Maulana Jalaluddin Rumi,* 1207–1273
>translated from Persian by Annemarie Schimmel

◑

Evening Hymn

O Christ, Son of the living God,
May your holy angels guard our sleep.
May they watch us as we rest
And hover around our beds.

Let them reveal to us in our dreams
Visions of your glorious truth,
O High Prince of the universe,
O High Priest of the mysteries.

May no dreams disturb our rest
And no nightmares darken our dreams.

May no fears or worries delay
Our willing, prompt repose.

May the virtue of our daily work
Hallow our nightly prayers.
May our sleep be deep and soft,
So our work be fresh and hard.

attributed to St. Patrick, c. 389–461

At Evening

I thank you, O God, for your care and protection this day,
keeping me from physical harm and spiritual corruption.
I now place the work of the day into your hands, trusting
that you will redeem my errors and turn my achievements
to your glory. And I now ask you to work within me, trust-
ing that you will use the hours of rest to create in me a new
heart and new soul. Let my mind, which through the day
has been directed to my work, through the evening be
wholly directed at you.

Jacob Boehme, 1575–1624

Be Thou My Vision

Be Thou my vision, O Lord of my heart;
Naught be all else to me, save that Thou art—
Thou my best thought by day or by night,
Waking or sleeping, Thy presence my light.

Riches I heed not, nor man's empty praise,
Thou mine inheritance, now and always;
Thou and Thou only, first in my heart,
High King of Heaven, my treasure Thou art.

High King of Heaven, after victory won,
May I reach heaven's joys, O bright heaven's Sun!
Heart of my own heart, whatever befall,
Still be my Vision, O ruler of all.

Mary Byrne, 1880–1931
from ancient Irish

Prayer

Prayer, the Church's banquet, Angels' age,
God's breath in man returning to his birth,
The soul in paraphrase, heart in pilgrimage,
The Christian plummet sounding heaven and earth;

Engine against the Almighty, sinner's tower,
    Reversèd thunder, Christ-side-piercing spear,
    The six-days' world transposing in an hour,
A kind of tune, which all things hear and fear;
Softness, and peace, and joy, and love, and bliss,
    Exalted Manna, gladness of the best,
    Heaven in ordinary, man well drest,
The milky way, the bird of Paradise,
    Church-bells beyond the stars heard, the soul's blood,
    The land of spices; something understood.

        George Herbert, 1593–1633

A Nocturnal Reverie

In such a *Night,* when every louder Wind
Is to its distant Cavern safe confin'd;
And only gentle *Zephyr* fans his Wings,
And lonely *Philomel,* still waking, sings;
Or from some Tree, fam'd for the *Owl's* delight,
She, hollowing clear, directs the Wand'rer right:
In such a *Night,* when passing Clouds give place,
Or thinly vail the Heav'ns mysterious Face;
When in some River, overhung with Green,
The waving Moon and trembling Leaves are seen;

When freshen'd Grass now bears itself upright,
And makes cool Banks to pleasing Rest invite,
Whence springs the *Woodbind,* and the *Bramble*-Rose,
And where the sleepy *Cowslip* shelter'd grows;
Whilst now a paler Hue the *Foxglove* takes,
Yet checquers still with Red the dusky brakes
When scatter'd *Glow-worms,* but in Twilight fine,
Shew trivial Beauties watch their Hour to shine;
Whilst *Salisb'ry* stands the Test of every Light,
In perfect Charms, and perfect Virtue bright:
When Odours, which declin'd repelling Day,
Thro' temp'rate Air uninterrupted stray;
When darken'd Groves their softest Shadows wear,
And falling Waters we distinctly hear;
When thro' the Gloom more venerable shows
Some ancient Fabrick, awful in Repose,
While Sunburnt Hills their swarthy Looks conceal,
And swelling Haycocks thicken up the Vale:
When the loos'd *Horse* now, as his Pasture leads,
Comes slowly grazing thro' th' adjoining Meads,
Whose stealing Pace, and lengthen'd Shade we fear,
Till torn up Forage in his Teeth we hear:
When nibbling *Sheep* at large pursue their Food,
And unmolested Kine rechew the Cud;
When *Curlews* cry beneath the Village-walls,
And to her straggling Brood the *Partridge* calls;

Their shortliv'd Jubilee the Creatures keep,
Which but endures, whilst Tyrant-*Man* do's sleep;
When a sedate Content the Spirit feels,
And no fierce Light disturb, whilst it reveals;
But silent Musings urge the Mind to seek
Something, too high for Syllables to speak;
Till the free Soul to a compos'dness charm'd,
Finding the Elements of Rage disarm'd,
O'er all below a solemn Quiet grown,
Joys in th' inferior World, and thinks it like her Own:
In such a *Night* let Me abroad remain,
Till Morning breaks, and All's confus'd again;
Our Cares, our Toils, our Clamours are renew'd,
Or Pleasures, seldom reach'd, again pursu'd.

Anne Finch, Countess of Winchilsea, 1661–1720

Night

The sun descending in the west,
The evening star does shine;
The birds are silent in their nest,
And I must seek for mine.

The moon like a flower
In heaven's high bower,

With silent delight
Sits and smiles on the night.

Farewell, green fields and happy groves,
Where flocks have took delight.
Where lambs have nibbled, silent moves
The feet of angels bright;
Unseen they pour blessing
And joy without ceasing,
On each bud and blossom,
And each sleeping bosom.

They look in every thoughtless nest,
Where birds are cover'd warm;
They visit caves of every beast,
To keep them all from harm.
If they see any weeping
That should have been sleeping,
They pour sleep on their head,
And sit down by their bed.

When wolves and tygers howl for prey,
They pitying stand and weep;
Seeking to drive their thirst away,
And keep them from the sheep;
But if they rush dreadful,
The angels, most heedful,
Receive each mild spirit,
New worlds to inherit.

And there the lion's ruddy eyes
Shall flow with tears of gold,
And pitying the tender cries,
And walking round the fold,
Saying "Wrath, by his meekness,
"And by his health, sickness
"Is driven away
"From our immortal day.

"And now beside thee, bleating lamb,
"I can lie down and sleep;
"Or think on him who bore thy name,
"Graze after thee and weep.
"For, wash'd in life's river,
"My bright mane for ever
"Shall shine like the gold
"As I guard o'er the fold."

William Blake, 1757–1827

Vespers

Hail, gladdening Light, of his pure glory poured
Who is the immortal Father, heavenly, blest,
Holiest of Holies, Jesus Christ our Lord!
Now we are come to the sun's hour of rest,

The lights of evening round us shine,
We hymn the Father, Son, and Holy Spirit divine.
Worthiest art thou at all times to be sung
With undefiled tongue,
Son of our God, giver of life, alone:
Therefore in all the world thy glories, Lord, we own.

Eastern Orthodox prayer

Even at Prayer

Even at prayer, our eyes look inward;
If the gate to the holy is shut, we just turn away.

The One is only the One, everyone knows—
What mirroring icon could hold it face to face?

Held back unvoiced, grief bruises the heart;
Not reaching the river, a raindrop is swallowed by dust.

If a story brings only tears and not blood to the eyes,
It is simply a lover's tale.

Whoever can't see the whole in every part plays at blind
     man's buff;
A wise man tastes the entire Tigris in every sip.

Ghalib, 1797–1869
translated from Urdu by Jane Hirshfield

Evening Prayer

Art thou abroad on this stormy night on the journey of love,
    my friend?
    The sky groans like one in despair.
I have no sleep to-night. Ever and again I open my door and
    look out
    on the darkness, my friend!
I can see nothing before me. I wonder where lies my path!
By what dim shore of the ink-black river, by what far edge of
    the frowning
    forest, through what mazy depth of gloom art thou
        threading thy course
    to come to me, my friend?

In the night of weariness let me give myself up to sleep
    without struggle, resting my trust upon thee.
Let me not force my flagging spirit into a poor preparation
    for thy worship.
It is thou who drawest the veil of night upon the tired eyes
    of the day to renew its sight in a fresher gladness of
    awakening.

Rabindranath Tagore, 1861–1941
translated from Bengali by the author

Baruch Spinoza

Like golden mist, the west lights up
The window. The diligent manuscript
Awaits, already laden with infinity.
Someone is building God in the twilight.
A man engenders God. He is a Jew
Of sad eyes and citrine skin.
Time carries him as the river carries
A leaf in the downstream water.
No matter. The enchanted one insists
And shapes God with delicate geometry.
Since his illness, since his birth,
He goes on constructing God with the word.
The mightiest love was granted him
Love that does not expect to be loved.

Jorge Luis Borges, 1899–1986
translated from Spanish by Yirmiyahu Yovel

I Can See in the Midst of Darkness

I can see that in the midst of darkness light persists. Hence
I gather that God is Life, Truth, Light. He is Love. He is the
Supreme Good. . . .

Prayer needs no speech. It is in itself independent of any sensuous effort. I have not the slightest doubt that prayer is an unfailing means of cleansing the heart of passions. But it must be combined with the utmost humility.

As food is necessary for the body, prayer is necessary for the soul. Prayer is an impossibility without a living faith in the presence of God within. God demands nothing less than complete self-surrender as the price for the only real freedom that is worth having.

Never own defeat in a sacred cause. Make up your mind henceforth that you will be pure and that you will find a response from God. But God never answers the prayers of the arrogant, nor the prayers of those who bargain with Him. If you would ask Him to help you, go to Him in all your nakedness; approach Him without reservations, also without fear or doubts as to how He can help a fallen being like you.

The prayer of even the most impure will be answered. I am telling this out of my personal experience, I have gone through the purgatory.

Prayer is the key of the morning and the bolt of the evening. "It is better in prayer to have a heart without words than words without a heart." [Bunyan]

I am giving you a bit of my experience and that of my companions when I say that he who has experienced the magic of prayer may do without food for days together but not for a single moment without prayer. For without prayer there is no inward peace.

The more my faith in God increased, the more irresistible became the yearnings for prayer. Life seemed to me dull and vacant without it. In fact food for the body is not so necessary as prayer for the soul.

I have found people who envy my peace. That peace comes from prayer; I am not a man of learning but I humbly claim to be a man of prayer. I am indifferent as to the form. Everyone is a law unto himself in that respect. . . .

After I had practiced silence for some time I saw the spiritual value of it. It suddenly flashed across my mind that that was the time when I could best hold communion with God.

Let everyone try and find out that as a result of daily prayer he adds something new to his life, something with which nothing else can be compared.

Mahatma Gandhi, 1869–1948

◑

Afterwards

When the Present has latched its postern behind my
    tremulous stay,
And the May month flaps its glad green leaves like wings,

Delicate-filmed as new-spun silk, will the neighbours say,
"He was a man who used to notice such things"?

If it be in the dusk when, like an eyelid's soundless blink,
The dewfall-hawk comes crossing the shades to alight
Upon the wind-warped upland thorn, a gazer may think,
"To him this must have been a familiar sight."

If I pass during some nocturnal blackness, mothy and warm,
When the hedgehog travels furtively over the lawn,
One may say, "He strove that such innocent creatures
        should come to no harm,
But he could do little for them; and now he is gone."

If, when hearing that I have been stilled at last, they stand at
        the door,
Watching the full-starred heavens that winter sees,
Will this thought rise on those who will meet my face no
        more,
"He was one who had an eye for such mysteries"?

And will any say when my bell of quittance is heard in the
        gloom,
And a crossing breeze cuts a pause in its outrollings,
Till they rise again, as they were a new bell's boom,
"He hears it not now, but used to notice such things"?

Thomas Hardy, 1840–1928

A Hymn to the Night

Once, when I poured out bitter tears, when my hope dissolved in pain and scattered, and I was standing alone at the barren hill which hid the shape of my life in its narrow, dark space—alone, as no one could be more alone, driven by unspeakable anxiety—strengthless, with just one thought left of need.—As I looked around for help, could not look forwards and not backwards, and hung on fleeting, extinguished life with infinite craving:—then came from blue distances—from the peaks of my old blessedness, a twilight spectacle—and with one stroke my birth's bond ripped—Light's chains. There the earthy splendor fled and sadness with it—misery flowed into a new, unplumbed world—You, Night-inspiration, heaven's sleep, came over me—the region lifted slowly up; over the region my released and newborn spirit floated. The hill became a cloud of dust—through the cloud I saw the transfigured features of my beloved. In her eyes rested the forever—I took her hands, and my tears were a glittering and unrippable bond. Years by the thousands flew off to the distance, like storms. On her neck I wept overjoyed tears at the new life.—It was the first and the only dream—and just since then I've felt an unchangeable, eternal faith in the heaven of Night and its Light, the beloved.

Novalis, 1772–1801
translated from German by Dick Higgins

from Thoughts in Solitude

When I am liberated by silence, when I am no longer
involved in the measurement of life, but in the living of it,
I can discover a form of prayer in which there is effectively,
no distraction. My whole life becomes a prayer. My whole
silence is full of prayer. The world of silence in which I am
immersed contributes to my prayer. . . .

Let me seek, then, the gift of silence, and poverty, and
solitude, where everything I touch is turned into prayer:
where the sky is my prayer, the birds are my prayer, the
wind in the trees is my prayer, for God is all in all.

Thomas Merton, 1915–1968

Nocturn

Night comes, an angel stands
Measuring out the time of stars,
Still are the winds, and still the hours.

It would be peace to lie
Still in the still hours at the angel's feet,
Upon a star hung in a starry sky,
But hearts another measure beat.

Each body, wingless as it lies,
Sends out its butterfly of night
With delicate wings and jewelled eyes.

And some upon day's shores are cast,
And some in darkness lost
In waves beyond the world, where float
Somewhere the islands of the blest.

Kathleen Raine

Among the Sounds of the Night

On the rough wet grass of the back yard my father and
mother have spread quilts. We all lie there, my mother, my
father, my uncle, my aunt, and I too am lying there. First we
were sitting up, then one of us lay down, and then we all lay
down, on our stomachs, or on our sides, or on our backs, and
they have kept on talking.

They are not talking much, and the talk is quiet, of noth-
ing in particular, of nothing at all in particular, of nothing at
all. The stars are wide and alive, they seem each like a smile
of great sweetness, and they seem very near. All my people
are larger bodies than mine, quiet, with voices gentle and
meaningless like the voices of sleeping birds. One is an
artist, he is living at home. One is a musician, she is living

at home. One is my mother who is good to me. One is my father who is good to me. By some chance, here they are, all on this earth; and who shall ever tell the sorrow of being on this earth, lying on quilts, on the grass, in a summer evening, among the sounds of the night. May God bless my people, my uncle, my aunt, my mother, my good father, oh, remember them kindly in their time of trouble; and in the hour of their taking away.

After a little I am taken in and put to bed. Sleep, soft smiling, draws me unto her: and those receive me, who quietly treat me, as one familiar and well-beloved in that home: but will not, oh, will not, not now, not ever; but will not ever tell me who I am.

James Agee, 1909–1955

◗

Thanks

Listen
with the night falling we are saying thank you
we are stopping on the bridges to bow from the railings
we are running out of the glass rooms
with our mouths full of food to look at the sky
and say thank you
we are standing by the water looking out
in different directions

back from a series of hospitals back from a mugging
after funerals we are saying thank you
after the news of the dead
whether or not we knew them we are saying thank you
looking up from the tables we are saying thank you
in a culture up to its chin in shame
living in the stench it has chosen we are saying thank you

over telephones we are saying thank you
in doorways and in the backs of cars and in elevators
remembering wars and the police at the back door
and the beatings on stairs we are saying thank you
in the banks that use us we are saying thank you
with the crooks in office with the rich and fashionable
unchanged we go on saying thank you thank you

with the animals dying around us
our lost feelings we are saying thank you
with the forests falling faster than the minutes
of our lives we are saying thank you
with the words going out like cells of a brain
with the cities growing over us like the earth
we are saying thank you faster and faster
with nobody listening we are saying thank you
we are saying thank you and waving
dark though it is

W. S. Merwin

Faith

I want to write about faith
    about the way the moon rises
        over cold snow, night after night,

faithful even as it fades from fullness,
    slowly becoming that last curving and impossible
        sliver of light before the final darkness.

But I have no faith myself
    I refuse it the smallest entry.

Let this then, my small poem,
    like a new moon, slender and barely open,
        be the first prayer that opens me to faith.

      David Whyte

Listening

My father could hear a little animal step,
or a moth in the dark against the screen,
and every far sound called the listening out
into places where the rest of us had never been.

More spoke to him from the soft wild night
than came to our porch for us on the wind;

we would watch him look up and his face go keen
till the walls of the world flared, widened.

My father heard so much that we still stand
inviting the quiet by turning the face,
waiting for a time when something in the night
will touch us too from that other place.

William Stafford, 1914–1993

Summer Night

The moon is nearly full,
      the humid air sweet like melon.
Flowers that have cupped the sun all day
      dream of iridescent wings
under the long dark sleep.
      Children's invisible voices call out
in the glimmering moonlight.
      Their parents play worn-out records
of the cumbia. Behind the screen door
      their soft laughter swells
into the rhythm of a smooth guitar.
      I watch the world shimmer
inside this globe of a summer night,
      listen to the wobble of her

spin and dive. It happens all the time, waiting for you

to come home.

There is an ache that begins

in the sound of an old blues song.

It becomes a house where all the lights have gone out

but one.

And it burns and burns

until there is only the blue smoke of dawn

and everyone is sleeping in someone's arms

even the flowers

even the sound of a thousand silences.

And the arms of night

in the arms of day.

Everyone except me.

But then the smell of damp honeysuckle twisted on the vine.

And the turn of the shoulder

of the ordinary spirit who keeps watch

over this ordinary street.

And there you are, the secret

of your own flower of light

blooming in the miraculous dark.

Joy Harjo

Night Game

Only bores are bored,—wrote William Saroyan—
And I was a bore, and so I went to the ball game;
But there was a pest who insisted on going with me.
I thought I could shake him if I bought one ticket,
But he must have come in on a pass. I couldn't see him,
But I knew he was there, back of third, in the row
    behind me,
His knees in my back, and his breath coming over my
    shoulder,
The loud-mouthed fool, the sickly nervous ego,
Repeating his silly questions, like a child
Or a girl at the first game ever. *Shut up,* I told him,
For Christ's sweet sake, shut up, and watch the ball game.
He didn't want to, but finally subsided,
And my attention found an outward focus,
Visible, pure, objective, inning by inning,
A well-played game, with no particular features,—
Feldman pitched well, and Ott hit a couple of homers.

And after the ninth, with the crowd in the bleachers
    thinning,
And the lights in the grandstand dimming out behind us,
And a full moon hung before us, over the clubhouse,
I drifted out with the crowd across the diamond,

Over the infield brown and the smooth green outfield,
So wonderful underfoot, so right, so perfect,
That each of us was a player for a moment,
The men my age, and the soldiers and the sailors,
Their girls, and the running kids, and the plodding old men,
Taking it easy, the same unhurried tempo,
In the mellow light and air, in the mild cool weather,
Moving together, moving out together,
Oh, this is good, I felt, to be part of this movement,
This mood, this music, part of the human race,
Alike and different, after the game is over,
Streaming away to the exit, and underground.

       Rolfe Humphries

◐

Evening Ritual

That night my wife and I as usual took our coffee out onto
the open porch in front of the house. We sat in silence
watching as the darkness brought the trees around the pond
into profile. Charlie performed his evening ritual of appear-
ing just before dark, sitting between us with his eyes alertly
fixed on the shutters where the bats were making their
little sounds of preparation. For a while we could hear the

children's voices from the bedrooms upstairs. Slowly the pauses got longer then they too entered the larger circle of our quiet.

I stood, touched my wife briefly, started to explain what I needed to do then realized an explanation wasn't necessary. I walked down the lawn toward the pond.

"Honey," Alice said softly.

"Yes?"

"I love you."

There was still enough light around the pond to tell whether the fish had bellied up. I leaned against the old beaver stump and studied the surface of the water. Soon the night speakers began declaring their thousand knowledges. Then there was no light but starlight. The Corona Borealis was near its zenith, Venus was dominant in the south, Orion was riding the dark ridge of pines behind me.

Suddenly everything went still as though some coded message had made listeners of us all. I heard something moving on the opposite bank. But then I wasn't sure. I held my breath to hear better. A presence. Deer? Raccoon? The great horned owl? The creature tongues resumed and I strained harder at the silence behind them. Then I knew I would never know.

James P. Carse

Knowing the Prayer

When the great Rabbi Israel Baal Shem-Tov saw misfortune threatening the Jews it was his custom to go into a certain part of the forest to meditate. There he would light a fire, say a special prayer, and the miracle would be accomplished and the misfortune averted. Later, when his disciple, the celebrated Magid of Mezritch, had occasion, for the same reason, to intercede with heaven, he would go to the same place in the forest and say: "Master of the Universe, listen! I do not know how to light the fire, but I am still able to say the prayer," and again the miracle would be accomplished. Still later, Rabbi Moshe-Leib of Sasov, in order to save his people once more, would go into the forest and say: "I do not know how to light the fire, I do not know the prayer, but I know the place and this must be sufficient." It was sufficient and the miracle was accomplished. Then it fell to Rabbi Israel of Rizhyn to overcome misfortune. Sitting in his armchair, his head in his hands, he spoke to God: "I am unable to light the fire and I do not know the prayer; I cannot even find the place in the forest. All I can do is to tell the story, and this must be sufficient." And it was sufficient.

God made man because he loves stories.

Elie Wiesel

Blue Mosque Reverie

A white crescent moon passes behind the long slope of
Sultan Ahmet's mosque, suddenly glazing ancient Istanbul
with silver light. The medieval stone archway in the pine-
bowered garden frames the six needle-shaped minarets and
twenty-four smaller domes like a bold border in an illumi-
nated manuscript.

In and out of the god-source dark night fly great white
streaks of seagulls, as if retracing the arabesque patterns on
the mosque. Near the jasmine-scented garden walls, a
peacock cries like a sleepless baby, a cry, the ancient Sufis
believed, for the soul to dance. From the cafes along the
labyrinthine lanes of the old city echoes the percussive
sound of slapping dominoes and a haunting of Turkish folk
songs that crackle on old radios.

In that deep pool of listening, I heard the dark conso-
nants of long-forgotten tongues and the sultan's horses
scraping prayers on old cobblestones wet with rain. It was
long ago that this would happen again.

Phil Cousineau

Night and Sleep

At the time of night-prayer, as the sun slides down,
the route the senses walk on closes, the route to the invisible
   opens.

The angel of sleep then gathers and drives along the spirits;
just as the mountain keeper gathers his sheep on a slope.

And what amazing sights he offers to the descending sheep!
Cities with sparkling streets, hyacinth gardens, emerald
   pastures!

The spirit sees astounding beings, turtles turned to men,
men turned to angels, when sleep erases the banal.

I think one could say the spirit goes back to its old home;
it no longer remembers where it lives, and loses its fatigue.

It carries around in life so many griefs and loads
and trembles under their weight; they are gone, it is all well.

Maulana Jalaluddin Rumi, 1207–1273
translated from Persian by Coleman Barks and Robert Bly

To Sleep, Perchance, to Dream

Darkly, the night encircles. Overhead, the moon glides on. Below, the earth rumbles. To bed, perhaps to sleep? To sleep, perchance, to dream? To dream, possibly to wake?

The desire for "sleep such as makes darkness brief," as the classical philosopher Martial remarked, is universal. People everywhere wish to know what will lure "sweet sleep" such as Odysseus and Penelope enjoyed after their twenty-year travail—sleep "that loosens the limbs of men . . . loosening the cares of the heart." The psalms promise peaceful slumber will come when you "commune with your own heart upon your bed and be still." For the serene John Keats, sleep was the "soft closer of our eyes." And the somnambulist Anthony Burgess once wrote from experience, "Sleep is gentle rocking travel along the river of dark."

So greatly have people searched through the ages for a comfortable bed and a good night's rest that enchanted sleepers are legendary. There are the Seven Sleepers of Ephesus, Rip Van Winkle, Merlin, and the hypersomniac Oblomov, who lent his name to a whole generation of soporific Russian students who snugly refused to get out of bed at all. Even nappers are part of the folklore. One of Thomas Edison's lesser known inventions was what we now call the "power nap."

Notorious for being able to flourish on two hours of sleep a night, Edison frequently stole catnaps under the laboratory tables. His naps illustrate the difference between long . . . restless . . . nights . . . and short but sound snoozing.

But in an anxious age where *rest* is a four-letter word and sleep to many accelerated souls often means only wasted time, how do we relearn the ancient *ars somnus,* the art of sleeping? What are the great sleep tonics? Reading mystery novels? Listening to late-night ball games? Drinking hot toddies? Drifting away on the sea of love's gentle currents? In this section we explore how ritualistic is the very notion of retiring for the night, how magical the beckoning of sleep, how exquisite the enigma of dream. And how timeless the connection between night, sleep, and love.

The sixth-century Greek philosopher Pythagoras could have been writing yesterday when he described the tentative moments before dozing off as the time for "daily action to be scanned." Reading how Leonardo believed it was advantageous "on finding oneself in bed in the dark to go over again in the imagination" the ideas of the day allows us to identify with a Renaissance man on at least one level. In an extract from Thomas De Quincey's book about the last days of Immanuel Kant, the nightly ritual of the "self-involved" philosopher who swathed himself in quilts "like a mummy, or . . . like the silkworm in its cocoon" sheds new light on the phrase "tightly wound."

Dream is a riddle wrapped inside the mystery of sleep inside the enigma of night, to paraphrase Winston Churchill. Few have handled the pieces of the puzzle of the soul as adeptly as poet Antonio

Machado. "Last Night I Had a Dream" is at once an invocation to storytime and a poem of incantatory images that evoke the "blessed illusion" of a poet's nightscapes. Thoreau's delphic revelation on the river came about because, he believed, "dreams are the touchstones of our characters."

"No one suspects the days to be gods," Emerson once said. Does anyone suspect the nights to be goddesses? In classical mythology Night was personified with sweet symmetry as the mother of Eros, that god of love who makes ecstatic the darkness. For Juan Ramón Jiménez, the love of his life is portrayed in "When, with You Asleep . . ." as giving him "the secret of the center / of the heavens." In Glenn Ingersoll's poem, "Winged Man," the divine and the erotic are indivisible. Through his lover's black eyes he sees "the night I am in amongst stars." Then in a marvelous leap, he imagines the Lord dreaming, "And I think that it pleases you, dreaming us upward." Sharon Olds, in her exquisitely observed poem, "Looking at Them Asleep," while watching her children's every move in their late-night slumber, hears the very voice of love ask her what she *knows*. Such a heart-stopping question—but she knows instantaneously, ". . . oh my Lord how I / know these two."

The splendid secrets of heaven and earth and the love that binds the two are reminiscent of the dream dance song of the California Wintu tribe,

> Where will you and I sleep?
> At the down-turned jagged rim of the sky you
> and I will sleep.

Let Sleep Not Come upon Thy Languid Eyes

Let sleep not come upon thy languid eyes
Before each daily action thou hast scanned;
What's done amiss, what done, what left undone;
From first to last examine all, and then
Blame what is wrong, in what is right rejoice.

attributed to Pythagoras, 6th century B.C.E.

●

from The Discourses

When the need of each opinion comes, we ought to have it
in readiness: on the occasion of breakfast, such opinions as
relate to breakfast; in the bath those that concern the bath;
in the bed, those that concern the bed.

Epictetus, fl. 100
translated by George Long

●

Benefits of the Dark

I have proved in my own case that it is of no small benefit
on finding oneself in bed in the dark to go over again in
the imagination the main outlines of the forms previously

studied, or of other noteworthy speculations; and this exercise is entirely to be recommended and it is useful in fixing things in the memory.

Leonardo da Vinci, 1452–1519

Golden Slumbers

Golden slumbers kiss your eyes,
Smiles awake you when you rise:
Sleep, pretty wantons, do not cry,
And I will sing you a lullaby:
Rock them, rock them lullaby.

Thomas Dekker, 1572–1632

What an Excellent Thing Sleep Is

Do but consider what an excellent thing sleep is: it is so inestimable a jewel that, if a tyrant would give his crown for an hour's slumber, it cannot be bought: of so beautiful a shape is it, that though a man lie with an Empress, his heart cannot beat quite till he leaves her embracements to be at rest with the other: yea, so greatly indebted are we to this kinsman of death, that we owe the better tributary, half our life to him: and there is good cause why we should do: for sleep is the golden chain that ties health and our bodies together. Who complains of want? of wounds? of cares? of great men's oppressions? of captivity? whilst he sleepeth? Beggars in their beds take as much pleasure as kings: can we therefore surfeit of this delicate ambrosia?

Thomas Dekker, 1572–1632

Sonnet XXVII

Weary with toil, I haste me to my bed,
The dear repose for limbs with travel tired;
But then begins a journey in my head
To work my mind, when body's work's expired:
For then my thoughts, from far where I abide,
Intend a zealous pilgrimage to thee,
And keep my drooping eyelids open wide,
Looking on darkness which the blind do see:
Save that my soul's imaginary sight
Presents thy shadow to my sightless view,
Which like a jewel hung in ghastly night
Makes black night beauteous and her old face new.
    Lo, thus, by day my limbs, by night my mind,
    For thee, and for myself no quiet find.

William Shakespeare, 1564–1616

The Sweet Sleep of Penelope and Odysseus

Thus they spoke to one another; and meanwhile Eurynome and the nurse made ready the bed of soft coverlets by the light of blazing torches. But when they had busily spread the stout-built bed-stead, the old nurse went back to her chamber to lie down, and Eurynome, the maiden of the bed-chamber, led them on their way to the couch with a torch in her hands; and when she led them to the bridal chamber, she went back. And they then gladly came to the place of the couch that was theirs of old. But Telemachus and the neatherd and the swineherd stayed their feet from dancing, and stayed the woman, and themselves lay down to sleep throughout the shadowy halls.

But when the two had had their fill of the joy of love, they took delight in tales, speaking each to the other. She, the fair lady, told of all that she had endured in the halls, looking upon the destructive throng of the wooers, who for her sake slew many beasts, cattle and goodly sheep; and great store of wine was drawn from jars. But Zeus-born Odysseus recounted all the woes that he had brought on men, and all the toil that in his sorrow he had himself endured, and she was glad to listen, nor did sweet sleep fall upon her eyelids, till he had told her the tale.

He began by telling how at the first he overcame the Cicones, and then came to the rich land of the Lotus-eaters, and all that the Cyclops wrought, and how he made him pay the price for his mighty comrades, whom the Cyclops had eaten, and had shown no pity. Then how he came to Aeolus, who received him with a ready heart, and sent him on his way; but it was not yet his fate to come to his dear native land, nay, storm-wind caught him up again, and bore him over the teeming deep, groaning heavily. Next how he came to Telepylus of the Læstrygonians, who destroyed his ships and his well-greaved comrades one and all, and Odysseus alone escaped in his black ship. Then he told of all the wiles and craftiness of Circe, and how in his benched ship he had gone to the dank house of Hades to consult the spirit of Theban Teiresias, and had seen all his comrades and the mother who bore him and nursed him, when a child. And how he heard the voice of the Sirens, who sing unceasingly, and had come to the Wandering Rocks, and to dread Charybdis, and to Scylla, from whom never yet had men escaped unscathed. Then how his comrades slew the kine of Helios, and how Zeus, who thunders on high, smote his swift ship with a flaming thunder-bolt, and his goodly comrades perished all together, while he alone escaped the evil fates. And how he came to the isle Ogygis and to the nymph Calypso who kept him there in her hollow caves, yearning that he should be her husband, and tended him, and said that she would make him immortal and ageless all his days; yet she could never persuade the heart in his breast. Then how he came after many toils to the Phaeacians, who heartily showed him all honour, as if he were a god, and sent him in a ship to his dear native land, after giving him stores of bronze and gold and raiment. This was the end of the tale, he told, when sweet sleep, that loosens the limbs of men, leapt upon him, loosening the cares of the heart.

> *Homer,* 6th century B.C.E.?
> translated from ancient Greek by A. T. Murray

from Sleep and Poetry

As I lay in my bed slepe full unmete
Was unto me, but why that I ne might
Rest I ne wist, for there n'as earthly wight
[As I suppose] had more of hertis ese
Than I, for I n'ad sicknesse nor disese.
Chaucer

What is more gentle than a wind in summer?
What is more soothing than the pretty hummer
That stays one moment in an open flower,
And buzzes cheerily from bower to bower?
What is more tranquil than a musk-rose blowing
In a green island, far from all men's knowing?
More healthful than the leafiness of dales?
More secret than a nest of nightingales?

More serene than Cordelia's countenance?
More full of visions than a high romance?
What, but thee Sleep? Soft closer of our eyes!
Low murmurer of tender lullabies!
Light hoverer around our happy pillows!
Wreather of poppy buds, and weeping willows!
Silent entangler of a beauty's tresses!
Most happy listener! when the morning blesses
Thee for enlivening all the cheerful eyes
That glance so brightly at the new sun-rise.

But what is higher beyond thought than thee?
Fresher than berries of a mountain tree?
More strange, more beautiful, more smooth, more regal,
Than wings of swans, than doves, than dim-seen eagle?
What is it? And to what shall I compare it?
It has a glory, and naught else can share it:
The thought thereof is awful, sweet, and holy,
Chasing away all worldliness and folly;
Coming sometimes like fearful claps of thunder,
Or the low rumblings earth's regions under;
And sometimes like a gentle whispering
Of all the secrets of some wondrous thing
That breathes about us in the vacant air;
So that we look around with prying stare,
Perhaps to see shapes of light, aërial limning,
And catch soft floatings from a faint-heard hymning,

To see the laurel wreath, on high suspended,
That is to crown our name when life is ended.
Sometimes it gives a glory to the voice,
And from the heart up-springs, "Rejoice! Rejoice!"—
Sounds which will reach the Framer of all things,
And die away in ardent mutterings.

No one who once the glorious sun has seen,
And all the clouds, and felt his bosom clean
For his great Maker's presence, but must know
What 'tis I mean, and feel his being glow:
Therefore no insult will I give his spirit,
By telling what he sees from native merit.
....

Stop and consider! life is but a day;
A fragile dew-drop on its perilous way
From a tree's summit; a poor Indian's sleep
While his boat hastens to the monstrous steep
Of Montmorenci. Why so sad a moan?
Life is the rose's hope while yet unblown;
The reading of an ever-changing tale;
The light uplifting of a maiden's veil;
A pigeon tumbling in clear summer air;
A laughing school-boy, without grief or care,
Riding the springing branches of an elm. . . .

John Keats, 1795–1821

The Way to Lie in Bed

After the first sleep 'tis not amiss to lie on the left side, that the meat may the better descend; and sometimes again on the belly, but never on the back. Seven or eight hours is a competent time for a melancholy man to rest, as Crato thinks: but as some do, to lie in bed and not sleep, a day, or half a day together, to give assent to pleasing conceits and vain imagination, is in many ways pernicious. . . . He that sleeps in the day-time, or is in suspense, fear, anyway troubled in mind, or goes to bed upon a full stomach, may never hope for quiet rest in the night; *nac enim meritoria somnos admittunt,* as the poet saith; inns and such-like troublesome places are not for sleep; one calls "Ostler!" another, "Tapster!" one cries and shouts, another sings, whoops, halloos. . . .

Who not accustomed to such noises can sleep among them? He that will intend to take his rest must go to bed *animo securo, quieto et libero,* with a secure and composed mind, in a quiet place: *omnia noctis erunt placida composta quiete* (at night all will be hushed in calm tranquillity): and if that will not serve, or may not be obtained, to seek then such means as are requisite. To lie in clean linen and sweet; before he goes to bed, or in bed, to hear "sweet music," which Ficinus commends . . . or, as Jobertus . . . "to read some pleasant author till he be asleep, to have a basin of water still dropping by his bedside," or to lie near that pleasant murmur, *lene sonantis aqua* (of gently trickling water), some flood-gates, arches, falls of water, like London Bridge, or some continuate noise which may benumb the senses.

Robert Burton, 1577–1640

A Renaissance Remedy for Wasteful Sleeplessness

It often happens to melancholiacs, especially to those who are men of letters, that their brains become dried out, and they become weak from long nights of sleeplessness. Because there is nothing that increases black bile trouble more than prolonged sleeplessness, one must take great pains to find help for this problem. These people should eat lettuce after some of their meals, together with a little bread and a little saffron. They should drink pure wine after the lettuce, and they should not stay up working beyond that hour. When they go to bed, they should take this formula: take two parts white poppy-seed, one part lettuce seed, balsam, and saffron, a half dram of each, and six parts sugar. Dissolve and cook it all in poppy-juice. Eat two drams of this stuff, and at the same time drink some poppy-juice or wine.

You can also smear on your face and temples an oil of violets, and if you do not have any, use camphor; the same with milk and oil of almond, and violet water. Move the nostrils with the fragrance of saffron and camphor, and with clippings from sweet fruit trees. Go very easy on vinegar, but use a lot of rosewater.

Smooth your bed with the leaves of cool plants. Delight your ears with pleasant songs and sounds. You can dampen your head a lot with a little bath in some water in which perhaps you have cooked the fruits of poppies, lettuce, purslain, mallows, roses, vines, willow, and the leaves of reeds, adding camomile. Having sweetened your bathwater with all these things, get your whole body wet with it, including arms and legs.

Furthermore, it is especially good to drink milk mixed with sugar, on an empty stomach, of course, if the stomach will tolerate it. This dampening business works wonderfully for melancholiacs, even for those who get enough sleep. Remember that almond milk should be very familiar to your table.

Marsilio Ficino, 1433–1499
translated from Italian by Charles Boer

◖

Kant's Critique of Pure Sleeping

After the candles were brought, Kant prosecuted his studies till nearly ten o'clock. A quarter of an hour before retiring for the night, he withdrew his mind as much as possible from every class of thoughts which demanded any exertion or energy of attention, on the principle, that by stimulating him and exciting him too much, such thoughts would be apt to cause wakefulness; and the slightest interference with his customary hour of falling asleep was in the highest degree unpleasant to him. Happily, this was with him a very rare occurrence. He undressed himself without his servant's assistance; but in such an order and with such a Roman regard to decorum and the Greek το πρεπον that he was always ready at a moment's warning to make his appearance without embarrassment to himself or to others. This done, he lay down on a mattress, and wrapped himself up in a quilt, which in summer was always of cotton; in autumn, of wool; at the setting in of winter, he used both; and, against severe cold, he protected himself by one of eiderdown, of which the part which covered his shoulders was not stuffed with feathers, but padded, or rather wadded closely with layers of wool. Long practice had taught him a very dexterous mode of *nesting* and enswathing himself in the bedclothes. First of all, he sat down on the bedside; then with an agile motion he vaulted obliquely into his lair; next he drew one corner of the bed-clothes under his left shoulder, and passing it below his back brought it round so as to rest under his right shoulder; fourthly, by a particular *tour d'adresse,* he operated on the other corner in the same way; and finally contrived to roll it round his whole person. Thus,

swathed like a mummy, or self-involved like the silk-worm
in its cocoon, he awaited the approach of sleep, which gen-
erally came on immediately.

Thomas De Quincey, 1785–1859

Beethoven's Night Thoughts to His Immortal Beloved

Good morning, on July 7 [1801]

Though still in bed my thoughts go out to you, my Immor-
tal Beloved, now and then joyfully, then sadly, waiting to
learn whether or not fate will hear us. I can live only wholly
with you or not at all—yes, I am resolved to wander so long
away from you until I can fly to your arms and say that I am
really at home, send my soul enwrapped in you into the
land of spirits.—Yes, unhappily it must be so—you will be
the more resolved since you know my fidelity—to you, no
one can ever again possess my heart—none—never—Oh,
God! why is it necessary to part from one whom one so
loves and yet my life in W. [Vienna] is now a wretched life—
your love makes me at once the happiest and the unhappiest
of men—at my age, I need a steady, quiet life—can that be
under our conditions? My angel, I have just been told that
the mail coach goes every day—and I must close at once so
that you may receive the L. at once. Be calm, only by a calm

consideration of our existence can we achieve our purpose
to live together—be calm—love me—today—yesterday—
what tearful longings for you—you—you—my life—my
all—farewell—Oh continue to love me—never misjudge the
most faithful heart of your beloved L.

> ever thine
> ever mine
> ever for each other

Ludwig van Beethoven, 1770–1827
unsent letter to unidentified inamorata

◑

Going to Bed with Music

Half our days we pass in the shadow of the earth; and the
brother of death exacteth a third part of our lives. A good
part of our sleep is peered out with visions and fantastical
objects, wherein we are confessedly deceived. The day sup-
plieth us with truth; the night with fictions and falsehoods
which uncomfortably divide the natural account of our
beings. And, therefore, having passed the day in sober
labours and rational enquiries of truth, we are fain to betake
ourselves unto such a state of being, wherein the soberest
heads have acted all the monstrosities of melancholy, and
which unto open eyes are no better than folly and madness.

Happy are they that go to bed with grand music, like Pythagoras, or have ways to compose the fantastical spirit, whose unruly wanderings take off inward sleep, filling our heads with St. Anthony's visions, and the dreams of Lipara in the sober chamber of rest.

The association of ideas brought about by this conjunction of beds and music reminds us of the recommendation made by a musician of the period, with regard to the care of lutes—one Thomas Mace. In view of the difficulty of keeping them in tune and in good condition, he suggests that they should be kept in a bed which is in constant use. The efficacy of the treatment, it seems to us, depends on what you mean by "constant use," as Dr. Joad would say. One can imagine circumstances and conditions of constant use which might seriously impair the capacities of the frail and fragile instrument.

Sir Thomas Browne, 1605–1682

Bringing Sleep to Weary Bodies

Lord Jesus Christ, you are the gentle moon and joyful stars, that watch over the darkest night. You are the source of all peace, reconciling the whole universe to the Father. You are the source of all rest, calming troubled hearts, and bringing sleep to weary bodies. You are the sweetness that fills our minds with quiet joy, and can turn the worst nightmares into dreams of heaven. May I dream of your sweetness, rest in your arms, be at one with your Father, and be comforted in the knowledge that you always watch over me.

Erasmus, 1469–1536

At Night

O Lord God, who has given us the night for rest, I pray that in my sleep my soul may remain awake to you, steadfastly adhering to your love. As I lay aside my cares to relax and relieve my mind, may I not forget your infinite and unresting care for me. And in this way, let my conscience be at peace, so that when I rise tomorrow, I am refreshed in body, mind and soul.

John Calvin, 1509–1564

On Going to Bed

As my head rests on my pillow
Let my soul rest in your mercy.

As my limbs relax on my mattress,
Let my soul relax in your peace.

As my body finds warmth beneath the blankets,
Let my soul find warmth in your love.

As my mind is filled with dreams,
Let my soul be filled with visions of heaven.

Johann Freylinghausen, 1670–1739

from The Parted Lovers

Come, my beloved, let us go up that shining mountain, and
  sit together on that shining mountain; there we will
    watch
    the Sun go down in beauty from that shining place.
There we will sit, till the Night Traveler arises in beauty
  about the shining mountain; we will watch him as he
  climbs to the beautiful skies.
We will also watch the little Stars following their chief.
We will also watch the Northern Lights playing their game of
  ball in their cold, glistening country.
There we will sit, on the beautiful mountain, and listen to the
  Thunder beating his drum.
We will see the flashes from the lit pipe of the Lightning.
We will see the great Whirlwind race with Squall.
There we will sit, until all creatures drowse.
There we will hear the great Owl sing his usual song: "Go-to-
  sleep-all," and see all animals obey his call.

There we will sit in beauty on the mountain, and watch the
    small Stars in their sleepless flight.
They do not mind the song, "go-to-sleep-all"; neither will we
    mind it, but sit more closely together, and think of
    nothing but ourselves, on the beautiful mountain.
Again, the "go-to-sleep-all" will be heard, and the Night
    Traveler will come closer to warn us that all are
      sleeping,
    except ourselves and the little Stars.
They and their chief are coursing along, and our minds go
    with them.
Then the Owl sleeps; no more is heard "go-to-sleep-all";
    the Lightnings flash afar; the great pipe is going out; the
    Thunder ceases beating his drum; and though our bodies
    urge us to be sleeping, we sit in beauty still upon the
    shining mountain.

Abanaki Indian song
translated by John Reade

Night

The sun never stopped shining and the Cashinahua Indians
didn't know the sweetness of rest.

Badly in need of peace, exhausted by so much light, they
borrowed night from the mouse.

It got dark, but the mouse's night was hardly long enough for a bite of food and a smoke in front of the fire. The people had just settled down in their hammocks when morning came.

So then they tried out the tapir's night. With the tapir's night they could sleep soundly and they enjoyed the long and much-deserved rest. But when they awoke, so much time had passed that undergrowth from the hills had invaded their lands and destroyed their houses.

After a big search they settled for the night of the armadillo. They borrowed it from him and never gave it back.

Deprived of night, the armadillo sleeps during the daytime.

> *Eduardo Galeano*
> translated from Spanish by Cedric Belfage

◖

The Midnight Guest

Once in the frozen hours of night
While the Great Bear circled Arktouros
and mortals lay drugged with sleep,
Eros stood at my gate, knocking.

"Who is pounding on my door?" I said.
"You are splitting my dreams."
"Open up. I'm only a child.
Don't be alarmed," Eros called in.
"I'm dripping wet and lost
and the night is black and moonless."
Hearing his words I pitied him
and quickly lit a candle.
Opening a door I saw a boy
with bow, wings and quiver.
I sat him down by the fire
and warmed his hands with my own,
and squeezed water from his hair.
When he recovered from the cold
he said, "Let's test this bow.
Rain has weakened the string."
He drew and struck me square
in the groin like a gadfly.
He leapt up laughing with scorn:
"Stranger, let us be happy.
My bow is unharmed, but you
will have trouble in your heart."

attributed to Anacreon, 1st century B.C.E.–6th century C.E.
translated from ancient Greek by Willis Barnstone

Chuang Tzu's Dream

Once upon a time,
I, Chuang Tzu,
dreamt I was a butterfly,
fluttering hither and thither,
to all intents and purposes a butterfly.

I was conscious only of following my fancies as
    a butterfly,
and was unconscious
of my individuality as a man.

Suddenly I awakened,
and there I lay, myself again.

Now I do not know
whether I was then a man
dreaming I was a butterfly,

or whether I am now
a butterfly dreaming
I am a man.

Chuang Tzu, 369–286 B.C.E.
translated from Chinese by Lin Yutang

A Dream of Mountaineering

At night, in my dream, I stoutly climbed a mountain,
Going out alone with my staff of holly-wood.
A thousand crags, a hundred hundred valleys—
In my dream-journey none were unexplored
And all the while my feet never grew tired
And my step was as strong as in my young days.
Can it be that when the mind travels backward
The body also returns to its old state?
And can it be, as between body and soul,
That the body may languish, while the soul is still strong?
Soul and body—both are vanities:
Dreaming and waking—both alike unreal.
In the day my feet are palsied and tottering;
In the night my steps go striding over the hills.
As day and night are divided in equal parts—
Between the two, I *get* as much as I *lose*.

Po Chü-i, 772–846
translated from Chinese by Arthur Waley

Dance of the Spirits

When it was time to gather acorns, all the people of Kamak
left their houses empty and went up on Palomar Mountain.
An old man named Pautovak came up from the neighboring

village of Ahoya, and stopped at Kamak. Finding the village deserted, he decided he would stay all night and go on in the morning. He took one of the enormous storage baskets, *mushkwanish,* that was empty, inverted it over himself for shelter, and went to sleep.

Early during the night he heard the people call out the summons to a dance. He lay and listened. There were children among the people, little boys, and they came near the granary basket. The basket had a rip through which the toes of the old man were sticking out. "A spirit," yelled the boys, and ran away.

The old man could recognize the voices of men and women who had died long ago. He could hear the spirits talk and hear them laugh. One was Exwanyawish, the woman that was turned into a rock, and Piyevla, the man that scooped the rock with his fingers. Piyevla sang that night all the songs that had been his when alive.

The old man could hear the women's songs as they danced. He lay awake all night and listened; till at last, just before dawn, he could not wait any longer, but determined to see them for himself; so suddenly throwing off the basket, he said, "Hai, are you there?" and immediately all the spirits turned into a flock of birds and flew away; and the turtle-shell rattle they had used all night for the dancing he found where they had left it, but now it was nothing but a piece of soaproot.

Salvador Cuevas, Luiseño

I Fell Asleep

I fell asleep thinking of him,
and he came to me.
If I had known it was only a dream
I would never have awakened.

Ono No Komachi, 834–880
translated from Japanese by Kenneth Rexroth

Echo

Come to me in the silence of the night;
    Come in the speaking silence of a dream;
Come with soft rounded cheeks and eyes as bright
    As sunlight on a stream;
        Come back in tears,
O memory, hope, love of finished years.

O dream how sweet, too sweet, too bitter sweet,
    Whose wakening should have been in Paradise,
Where souls brimfull of love abide and meet;
    Where thirsting longing eyes
        Watch the slow door
That opening, letting in, lets out no more.

Yet come to me in dreams, that I may live
    My very life again though cold in death:
Come back to me in dreams, that I may give
    Pulse for pulse, breath for breath:
      Speak low, lean low,
As long ago, my love, how long ago.

Christina Rossetti, 1830–1894

The Vision to Electra

I dream'd we both were in a bed
Of Roses, almost smothered:
The warmth and sweetnes had me there
Made lovingly familiar:
But that I heard thy sweet breath say,
Faults done by night will blush by day:
I kist thee (panting) and I call
Night to the Record! that was all.
But ah! if empty dreames so please,
Love give me more such nights as these.

Robert Herrick, 1591–1674

The Visionary

Silent is the house: all are laid asleep:
One alone looks out o'er the snow-wreaths deep,
Watching every cloud, dreading every breeze
That whirls the 'wildering drift, and bends the
     groaning trees.

Cheerful is the hearth, soft the matted floor;
Not one shivering gust creeps through pane or door;
The little lamp burns straight, its rays shoot
     strong and far:
I trim it well, to be the wanderer's guiding-star.

Frown, my haughty sire! chide, my angry dame!
Set your slaves to spy; threaten me with shame:
But neither sire nor dame, nor prying serf shall know
What angel nightly tracks that waste of frozen snow.

What I love shall come like visitant of air,
Safe in secret power from lurking human snare;
Who loves me, no word of mine shall e'er betray,
Though for faith unstained my life must forfeit pay.

Burn then, little lamp; glimmer straight and clear—
Hush! a rustling wing stirs, methinks, the air:
He for whom I wait thus ever comes to me;
Strange Power! I trust thy might; trust thou
     my constancy.

Emily Brontë, 1818–1848

Last Night I Had a Dream

Last night I had a dream—
a blessed illusion it was—
I dreamt of a fountain flowing
deep down in my heart.
Water, by what hidden channels
have you come, tell me, to me,
welling up with new life
    I never tasted before?
Last night I had a dream—
a blessed illusion it was—
I dreamt of a hive at work
deep down in my heart.
Within were the golden bees
straining out the bitter past
to make sweet-tasting honey,
and white honeycomb.
    Last night I had a dream—
a blessed illusion it was—
I dreamt of a hot sun shining
deep down in my heart.
The heat was in the scorching
as from a fiery hearth;
the sun in the light it shed
and the tears it brought to the eyes.

> Last night I had a dream—
> a blessed illusion it was—
> I dreamed it was God I'd found
> deep down in my heart.

> *Antonio Machado,* 1875–1939
> translated from Spanish by Alan S. Youngblood

Lethe

Come to my breast, soul hard and passionless,
Beloved tiger, beast with languid airs;
I want to plunge my hands into your hair
Heavy and thick, in tremulous caress;

In petticoats all fragrant with your scent
Bury my aching and uneasy head,
And breathe in, like a flower long since dead,
The musty sweetness of my love now spent.

I want to sleep—to sleep rather than live!
In sleep as gentle as eternity,
I shall spread out my kisses ruthlessly
Upon your copper skin superlative.

I know of nowhere like your bed's abyss
To swallow up my agony, now gone;

Upon your lips dwells great oblivion,
And Lethe flows on in your every kiss.

My destiny is henceforth my delight,
And like a destined man I shall consent;
A docile martyr, victim innocent,
Whose very fervour makes the flames burn bright.

And I shall drink, to drown my bitterness,
Nepenthe and refreshing hellebore
From those sharp-pointed breasts that I adore,
Which never held a heart under duress.

Charles Baudelaire, 1821–1867
translated from French by Joanna Richardson

A Dream Within a Dream

Take this kiss upon the brow!
And, in parting from you now,
Thus much let me avow—
You are not wrong, to deem
That my days have been a dream;
Yet if hope has flown away
In a night, or in a day,
In a vision, or in none,

Is it therefore the less *gone*?
All that we see or seem
Is but a dream within a dream.

I stand amid the roar
Of a surf-tormented shore,
And I hold within my hand
Grains of the golden sand—
How few! yet how they creep
Through my fingers to the deep,
While I weep—while I weep!
O, God! can I not grasp
Them with a tighter clasp?
O, God! can I not save
One from the pitiless wave?
Is *all* that we see or seem
But a dream within a dream?

Edgar Allan Poe, 1809–1849

Meeting at Night

The gray sea and the long black land;
And the yellow half-moon large and low;
And the startled little waves that leap
In fiery ringlets from their sleep,

As I gain the cove with pushing prow,
And quench its speed in the slushy sand.

Then a mile of warm sea-scented beach;
Three fields to cross till a farm appears;
A tap at the pane, the quick sharp scratch
And blue spurt of a lighted match,
And a voice less loud, through its joys and fears,
Than the two hearts beating each to each!

Robert Browning, 1812–1889

◐

Dreaming by the River

WEDNESDAY: While we float here, far from that tributary stream on whose banks our friends and kindred dwell, our thoughts, like the stars, come out of their horizon still. After years of vain familiarity, some distant gesture or unconscious behavior, which we remember, speaks to us with more emphasis than the wisest or kindest words. We are sometimes made aware of a kindness long passed, and realize that there have been times when our friends' thoughts of us were of so pure and lofty a character that they passed over us like the winds of heaven unnoticed; when they treated us not as what we were, but as what we aspired to be. Friendship is evanescent in every man's experience, and remembered like heat lightning in past summers. Fair and flitting like a summer cloud—there is always some vapor in the air, no matter how long the drought.

We found a convenient harbor for our boat at the mouth of a small brook which emptied into the Merrimack. We sat on the bank eating our supper and we enjoyed so serene an evening as left nothing to describe. For the most part we think that there are few degrees of sublimity, and that the highest is but little higher than that which we now behold; but we are always deceived.

I dreamed this night of an event which had occurred long before. Dreams are the touchstones of our characters. We are scarcely less afflicted when we remember some unworthiness in our conduct in a dream, than if it had been actual. For in dreams we but act a part which must have been learned and rehearsed in our waking hours. Our truest life is when we are in dreams awake.

Henry David Thoreau, 1817–1862

The Chimney Sweeper

When my mother died I was very young,
And my father sold me while yet my tongue
Could scarcely cry "'weep! 'weep! 'weep! 'weep!"
So your chimneys I sweep, & in soot I sleep.

There's little Tom Dacre, who cried when his head,
That curl'd like a lamb's back, was shav'd: so I said
"Hush, Tom! never mind it, for when your head's bare
"You know that the soot cannot spoil your white hair."

And so he was quiet, & that very night,
As Tom was a-sleeping, he had such a sight!
That thousands of sweepers, Dick, Joe, Ned, & Jack,
Were all of them lock'd up in coffins of black.

And by came an Angel who had a bright key,
And he open'd the coffins & set them all free;
Then down a green plain leaping, laughing, they run,
And wash in a river, and shine in the Sun.

Then naked & white, all their bags left behind,
They rise upon clouds and sport in the wind;
And the Angel told Tom, if he'd be a good boy,
He'd have God for his father, & never want joy.

And so Tom awoke; and we rose in the dark,
And got with our bags & our brushes to work.
Tho' the morning was cold, Tom was happy & warm;
So if all do their duty they need not fear harm.

William Blake, 1757–1827

from The Sleepers

1

I wander all night in my vision,
Stepping with light feet, swiftly and noiselessly stepping
    and stopping,
Bending with open eyes over the shut eyes of sleepers,
Wandering and confused, lost to myself, ill-assorted,
    contradictory,
Pausing, gazing, bending, and stopping.

How solemn they look there, stretch'd and still,
How quiet they breathe, the little children in their cradles.
....

The married couple sleep calmly in their bed, he with his
    palm on the hip of his wife, and she with her palm on the
    hip of the husband,
The sisters sleep lovingly side by side in their bed,
The men sleep lovingly side by side in theirs,
And the mother sleeps with her little child carefully wrapt.
....

I go from bedside to bedside, I sleep close with the other
    sleepers each in turn,
I dream in my dream all the dreams of the other dreamers,
And I become the other dreamers.

I am a dance—play up there! the fit is whirling me fast!

8

....

I too pass from the night,
I stay a while away O night, but I return to you again and
      love you.
Why should I be afraid to trust myself to you?
I am afraid, I have been well brought forward by you,
I love the rich running day, but I do not desert her in
      whom I lay so long,
I know not how I came of you and I know not where I go
      with you, but I know I came well and shall go well.

I will stop only a time with the night, and rise betimes,
I will duly pass the day O my mother, and duly return
      to you.

Walt Whitman, 1819–1892

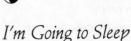

I'm Going to Sleep

Teeth of flowers, coif of dew,
hands of grasses, you, gentle nurse,
turn down the earthy sheets
and the eiderdown of weeded mosses.

I'm going to sleep, nurse, put me to bed.
Put a lamp at the headboard;
a constellation, whichever one you like;
they're all nice; turn it down a little.

Leave me alone: you can hear the tender shoots . . .
a celestial foot is rocking you from above
and a bird is tapping out some rhythms

so you can forget . . . Thank you . . . Oh yes, a message:
if he calls again on the phone
tell him not to keep trying, tell him I've gone out.

> *Alfonsina Storni,* 1892–1938
> 24th of October 1938
> translated from Spanish by Perry Higman

When, with You Asleep . . .

When, with you asleep, I plunge into your soul,
and I listen, with my ear
on your naked breast,
to your tranquil heart, it seems to me
that, in its deep throbbing, I surprise
the secret of the center
of the world.

It seems to me
that legions of angels
on celestial steeds
—as when, in the height
of the night we listen, without a breath
and our ears to the earth,
to distant hoofbeats that never arrive—,
that legions of angels
are coming through you, from afar
—like the Three Kings
to the eternal birth
of our love—,
they are coming through you, from afar,
to bring me, in your dreams,
the secret of the center
of the heavens.

Juan Ramón Jiménez, 1881–1958
translated from Spanish by Perry Higman

Falling Down Roads of Sleep

we are falling down roads into sleep
falling into sleep from blues

posing as the sky, the eye of the Creator, moves
black cataracts of clouds around, pointillistic, as clues
wet, as when a bad knee tells us that rain is coming
before night floods down the streets
sleep is seducing, as the light
slips from the night, slips from our eyes
& slides across the sky, like feet over ice
the lances of our intentions, glancing off moons
slicing the edge of noon
we remember a sky blue & deep with light
remember the wings of birds turning around hours
burning off suns, flights of music diving toward night
like warring elements, our speech thunderclapping
down streets lugubrious with sleep
deep down we leap, back into sleep, so steep
the fall back into blues
we forget the fading of night, coming
begin climbing up ladders of song, rung by rung
sleep falling between our language, now, lifting
toward flight, rain clouds, like circling crows
cruise under light, under the bold
gold polished coin of the sun, holding

Quincy Troupe

Sleep, Darling

Sleep, darling

I have a small
daughter called
Cleis, who is

like a golden
flower
    I wouldn't
take all Croesus'
kingdom with love
thrown in, for her

Sappho, 6th century B.C.E.
translated from ancient Greek by Mary Barnard

●

Sleep, Baby, Sleep

    Sleep, baby, sleep,
Our cottage vale is deep:
The little lamb is on the green,
With woolly fleece so soft and clean—
    Sleep, baby, sleep.
    Sleep, baby, sleep,

Down where the woodbines creep;
Be always like the lamb so mild,
A kind, and sweet, and gentle child
Sleep, baby, sleep.

from The Real Mother Goose

The Land of Nod

From breakfast on through all the day
At home among my friends I stay,
But every night I go abroad
Afar into the land of Nod.

All by myself I have to go,
With none to tell me what to do—
All alone beside the streams
And up the mountain-sides of dreams.

The strangest things are there for me,
Both things to eat and things to see,
And many frightening sights abroad
Till morning in the land of Nod.

Try as I like to find the way,
I never can get back by day,

Nor can remember plain and clear
The curious music that I hear.

Robert Louis Stevenson, 1850–1894

Humming Home Your Shadow

When you get up in the morning, Hoopa Indian children are
told, it is very important for you to wait until you get your
shadow home. When you go to sleep at night, part of you—
your shadow—takes off. The part that you've held down all
day, the part that you wouldn't let live. When you go to bed,
your shadow says, "Now is my chance. I will go out and
explore the world that you won't let me touch all day." And
off it goes. The shadow has the freedom to go as far away
as it wants to, but it has one tie: You have a hum that only
your shadow knows. And it can never disobey you. So when
you get up in the morning, if you remember to hum, your
shadow will come back home. Even though it doesn't want
to. So when you get up, before you go out, give your own
little hum, and your shadow will say, "Oh! I have to go
home," and it will come home. And you are never ready for
the day until you have taken time to sing the song of your
own shadow. Some people say, "I must have gotten up on
the wrong side of the bed—I think I'll go back and start

over." They've forgotten to hum! Or some people get up at
seven, and at ten o'clock they're still saying, "Don't mind
me, I'm not all here." They've forgotten to hum! So there is
a land of wisdom in remembering to get yourself all here
every day. This is taught to the Hoopa tribal children not by
saying, "When you get up in the morning you must do this!"
but by saying, "Hum your song, so your heart and your
spirit come together."

Hoopa Indian
retold by Sister Maria José Hobday

Looking at Them Asleep

When I come home late at night and go in to kiss the
    children,
I see my girl with her arm curled around her head,
her face deep in unconsciousness—so
deeply centered she is in her dark self,
her mouth slightly puffed like one sated but
slightly pouted like one who hasn't had enough,
her eyes so closed you would think they have rolled the
iris around to face the back of her head,
the eyeball marble-naked under that
thick satisfied desiring lid,

she lies on her back in abandon and sealed completion,
and the son in his room, oh the son he is sideways in his bed,
one knee up as if he is climbing
sharp stairs up into the night,
and under his thin quivering eyelids you
know his eyes are wide open and
staring and glazed, the blue in them so
anxious and crystally in all this darkness, and his
mouth is open, he is breathing hard from the climb
and panting a bit, his brow is crumpled
and pale, his long fingers curved,
his hand open, and in the center of each hand
the dry dirty boyish palm
resting like a cookie. I look at him in his
quest, the thin muscles of his arms
passionate and tense, I look at her with her
face like the face of a snake who has swallowed a deer,
content, content—and I know if I wake her she'll
smile and turn her face toward me though
half asleep and open her eyes and I
know if I wake him he'll jerk and say Don't and sit
up and stare about him in blue
unrecognition, oh my Lord how I
know these two. When love comes to me and says
What do you know, I say This girl, this boy.

Sharon Olds

Hearing My Prayers

for my mother & father

You taught my clumsy hands to form a steeple,
fingers pointing upward in the wish for wings
—little hands that swarmed with bugs
when I picked an eyeless wren up from a gutter.
You taught my knees to kneel,
prepared me to embark on darkness,
prepared me for bed: first and final altar
before which we are all acolytes
whispering *Suscipiat.** I fell asleep
hearing you awake in other rooms.

Now it's my turn to hear *your* prayers,
voices side by side, hands that quelled nightmares
folded forever. I'm listening.

Sleep tight. Don't let the bedbugs bite.
My soul to keep my soul to take
Now I lay me down to wake.
My goodnight kiss, this gentle gibberish.
I tuck you in, lay my hand on your heads.

*Suscipiat is Latin for "Receive." One of the altar boys' responses from the
Offertory of the Mass: "Receive O God this Sacrifice . . ."

Close your eyes, peer into darkness.
Don't be afraid. You will find each other,
you will love each other, and I will be born.

Jeff Poniewaz

◖

In No Way

I am of the family of the universe, and with all of us together
I do not fear being alone; I can reach out and touch a rock or
a hand or dip my feet in water. Always there is some body
close by, and when I speak I am answered by a plane's roar
or the bird's whistling or the voices of others in conversation
far apart from me. When I lie down to sleep, I am in the
company of the dark and the stars.

Breathe to me, sheep in the meadow. Sun and moon,
my father and my father's brother, kiss me on the brow with
your light. My sister, earth, holds me up to be kissed. Sun
and moon, I smile at you both and spread my arms in affec-
tion and lay myself down at full length for the earth to know
I love it too and am never to be separated from it. In no way
shall death part us.

David Ignatow

Sleeping, Turning in Turn like Planets

Sleeping, turning in turn like planets
rotating in their midnight meadow:
a touch is enough to let us know
we're not alone in the universe, even in sleep:
the dream-ghosts of two worlds
walking their ghost-towns, almost address each other.
I've wakened to your muttered words
spoken light- or dark-years away
as if my own voice had spoken.
But we have different voices, even in sleep,
and our bodies, so alike, are yet so different
and the past echoing through our bloodstreams
is freighted with different language, different meanings—
though in any chronicle of the world we share
it could be written with new meaning
we were two lovers of one gender,
we were two women of one generation.

Adrienne Rich

Sleeping Habit

Startled by a sharp pain, as if her hair were being pulled out,
she woke up three or four times. But when she realized that

a skein of her black hair was wound around the neck of her lover, she smiled to herself. In the morning, she would say, "My hair is this long now. When we sleep together, it truly grows longer."

Quietly, she closed her eyes.

"I don't want to sleep. Why do we have to sleep? Even though we are lovers, to have to go to sleep, of all things!" On nights when it was all right for her to stay with him, she would say this, as if it were a mystery to her.

"You'd have to say that people make love precisely because they have to sleep. A lover that never sleeps—the very idea is frightening. It's something thought up by a demon."

"That's not true. At first, we never slept either, did we? There's nothing so selfish as sleep."

That was the truth. As soon as he fell asleep, he would pull his arms out from under her neck, frowning unconsciously as he did so. She, too, no matter where she embraced him, would find when she awakened that the strength had gone out of her arm.

"Well, then, I'll wind my hair around and around your arm and hold you tight."

Winding the sleeve of his sleeping kimono around her arm, she'd held him hard. Just the same, sleep stole away the strength from her fingers.

"All right, then, just as the old proverb says, I'll tie you up with the rope of a woman's hair." So saying, she'd drawn a long skein of her raven-black hair around his neck.

That morning, however, he smiled at what she said.

"What do you mean, your hair has grown longer? It's so tangled up you can't pass a comb through it."

As time went by, they forgot about that sort of thing. These nights, she slept as if she'd even forgotten he was there. But, if she happened to wake up, her arm was always touching him—and his arm was touching her. By now, when they no longer thought about it, it had become their sleeping habit.

Yasunari Kawabata, 1899–1972
translated from Japanese by Lane Dunlop

And Now You're Mine

And now you're mine. Rest with your dream in my dream.
Love and pain and work should all sleep, now.
The night turns on its invisible wheels,
and you are pure beside me as a sleeping amber.

No one else, Love, will sleep in my dreams. You will go,
we will go together, over the waters of time.

No one else will travel through the shadows with me,
only you, evergreen, ever sun, ever moon.

Your hands have already opened their delicate fists
and let their soft drifting signs drop away;
your eyes closed like two gray wings, and I move

after, following the folding water you carry, that carries
me away. The night, the world, the wind spin out their
      destiny.
Without you, I am your dream, only that, and that is all.

Pablo Neruda, 1904–1973
translated from Spanish by Stephen Tapscott

◑

Wild Nights—Wild Nights!

Wild Nights—Wild Nights!
Were I with thee
Wild Nights should be
Our luxury!

Futile—the Winds—
To a Heart in port—
Done with the Compass—
Done with the Chart!

Rowing in Eden—
Ah, the Sea!
Might I but moor—Tonight—
In Thee!

Emily Dickinson, 1830–1886

Winged Man

Five, six times a second my heart fills,
fills and empties itself;
and what warms my lips comes from there.
What strengthens the bones of my wings passes through my
    heart.

I have a lover in whose black eyes I see the night,
the night I am in amongst stars.
Lord, the grip of your heaven is a relaxed grip,
as of a hand half sleeping,

as though, Lord, you were dreaming me up,
your dreaming keeping me aloft in his eyes,
the night in which my wings are strong.

Your mouth is parted, Lord, and it is a sleep word
you have spoken that none of us can remember.

Or it was laughter.
And I think that it pleases you, dreaming us upward.

Glenn Ingersoll

Fall of the Evening Star

Speak softly; sun going down
Out of sight. Come near me now.

Dear dying fall of wings as birds
Complain against the gathering dark . . .

Exaggerate the green blood in grass;
The music of leaves scraping space;

Multiply the stillness by one sound;
By one syllable of your name . . .

And all that is little is soon giant,
All that is rare grows in common beauty

To rest with my mouth on your mouth
As somewhere a star falls

And the earth takes it softly, in natural love . . .
Exactly as we take each other . . . and go to sleep.

Kenneth Patchen, 1911–1972

Sleeping on the Wing

Perhaps it is to avoid some great sadness,
as in a Restoration tragedy the hero cries "Sleep!
O for a long sound sleep and so forget it!"
that one flies, soaring above the shoreless city,
veering upward from the pavement as a pigeon
does when a car honks or a door slams, the door
of dreams, life perpetuated in parti-colored loves
and beautiful lies all in different languages.
Fear drops away too, like the cement, and you
are over the Atlantic. Where is Spain? where is
who? The Civil War was fought to free the slaves,
was it? A sudden down-draught reminds you of gravity
and your position in respect to human love. But
here is where the gods are, speculating, bemused.
Once you are helpless, you are free, can you believe
that? Never to waken to the sad struggle of a face?
to travel always over some impersonal vastness,
to be out of, forever, neither in nor for!

The eyes roll asleep as if turned by the wind
and the lids flutter open slightly like a wing.
The world is an iceberg, so much is invisible!
and was and is, and yet the form, it may be sleeping
too. Those features etched in the ice of someone
loved who died, you are a sculptor dreaming of space

and speed, your hand alone could have done this.
Curiosity, the passionate hand of desire. Dead,
or sleeping? Is there speed enough? And, swooping,
you relinquish all that you have made your own,
the kingdom of your self sailing, for you must awake
and breathe your warmth in this beloved image
whether it's dead or merely disappearing,
as space is disappearing and your singularity.

Frank O'Hara, 1926–1966

Burning the Midnight Oil

Not all nightbound souls go willingly into the arms of Morpheus. Some resist as if recalling a blood memory that the god of sleep is brother to the lord of death and his embrace must be avoided as long as possible. The Lunda people in Africa tell the "Sleep Test" myths, stories about the "little deaths" the gods have subjected human beings to every night because people haven't learned to stay awake. The word for *dream* in the Aztec language of Nahuatl is *temictli,* which means "the edge of death." In the Garden of Gethsemane, Jesus admonished the apostles, "Couldn't you stay awake?" On the streets of Konya, Rumi cajoled his avid followers, "The breeze at dawn has secrets to tell you. Don't go to sleep!" During Elizabethan times, a common gentleman's expression for going to sleep was being "buried in bed," a sepulchral thought embodied in Shakespeare's Macbeth, who speaks of sleep as the death of each day's life.

This part is composed of writers who swear by the proverb that "there will be sleep enough in the grave," or that "sleep is the greatest thief." These are travelers on the back roads of the night, night-combers searching for treasure on moon-starved beaches, restless souls who cleave to the possibility that there is a kind of crazy wisdom in the night air inaccessible by day. Their response to the threat of sleep is a formidable flurry of late-night activity. Their patron saint is Saint-Pol-Roux, who hung a sign on his door proclaiming "The poet is working" when his guard was down and he was forced to sleep. For these writers, dreamtime is the late shift of literature.

During the medieval ages, a popular image for this *carpe noctum,* this seizing of the night, came from alchemists, monks, and philosophers, leaning one elbow on an oak table and one hand on the *memento mori* skull, penning their fever-browed lucubrations until dawn. The fourteenth-century philosopher Petrarch voiced his insatiable appetite for nocturnal creativity: "It is remarkable that I long to write, yet do not know what to write, or to whom, and yet—what an unrelenting pleasure!—paper, pen, ink and sleepless nights give more satisfaction than sleep and repose."

Icons of our time include the scientist, poet, pilot, explorer, or musician staying up until dawn in the conviction that "night time is the right time," as Ray Charles moans in the key of midnight blue. The nightbird Robert Frost was "acquainted with the night," for he had "outwalked the furthest city light." While flying *West with the Night,* adventurer Beryl Markham later wrote she felt "irrevocably alone, with . . . nothing to contemplate but the size of [her] small courage," leading to the startling realization that she had been a stranger to herself until those moments. Naturalist John Muir was fond of rousing himself at midnight to tramp through the wilds, as he did once to encounter a moonlit Alaskan glacier, because "it seemed then a sad thing that any part of so precious a night had been lost in sleep." Poet

Kenneth Rexroth expresses both his genius and the vulnerability brought on by the late night in a chair before the fire when he writes in "Runaway," "I wish I could be sure that deep in you / Was a magnet to draw you always home."

These are hungers for the dark tones of life, the *duende* of the night; these are hopes for personal epiphany, searing self-realization, or an encounter with the luminous night. This squinting in the soul is for true vision, learning to see the invisible. For we strive always to see in the dark; we hope for light through poems and prayers; and we pay any cost to wedge open a crack between the worlds if it means learning one new thing about ourselves.

A sign on the door to one of the studios at a famous animation house warns:

> Don't open the door.
> The darkness may leak out.

Night Rules

> Abbot Lot came to Abbot Joseph and said: Father, according as I am able, I keep my little rule, and my little fast, my prayer, meditation and contemplative silence; and according as I am able I strive to cleanse my heart of thoughts: now what more should I do? The elder rose up in reply and

stretched out his hands to heaven, and his fingers became like ten lamps of fire. He said: Why not be totally changed into fire?

from the traditional sayings of the Desert Fathers, 4th century version by Thomas Merton

The Sentinel in Love

A soldier was in love. Even if not on guard he could never rest. At last, a friend begged him to have a few hours' sleep. The soldier said: "I am a sentinel, and I am in love. How can I rest? A soldier on duty must not sleep, so it is an advantage to him to be in love. Each night love puts me to the test, and thus I can stay awake and keep watch on the fort. This love is a friend to the sentinel, for wakefulness becomes part of him; he who reaches this state will ever be on the watch."

Do not sleep, O man, if you are striving for knowledge of yourself. Guard well the fortress of your heart, for there are thieves everywhere. Do not let brigands steal the jewel you carry. True knowledge will come to him who can stay awake. He who patiently keeps watch will be aware when God comes near him. True lovers who wish to surrender themselves to the intoxication of love go apart together. He who has spiritual love holds in his hand the keys of the two

worlds. If one is a woman one becomes a man; and if one is
a man one becomes a deep ocean.

Farid ud-Din Attar, 1110–1230
rendered into English by C. S. Nott
from the French translation of Garcin de Tassy

A Prayer to the Gods of Night

They are lying down, the Great Ones,
the bars have fallen, the bolts are shot,
the crowds and all the people rest,
the open gates are locked.
The gods of the land, the goddesses,
Shamash Sin Adad Ishtar,
sun, moon, turmoil, love
lie down to sleep in heaven.
The judgement seat is empty now,
for no god now is still at work.
Night has drawn down the curtain,
the temples and the sanctuaries are silent, dark.
Now the traveller calls to his god,
defendant and plaintiff sleep in peace,
for the judge of truth, the father of the fatherless,
Shamash, has gone to his chamber.
"O Great Ones, Princes of the Night,

Bright Ones, Gibil the furnace, Irra
war-lord of the Underworld,
Bow-star and Yoke, Orion, Pleiades, Dragon,
the Wild Bull, the Goat, and the Great Bear,
stand by me in my divination.
By this lamb that I am offering,
may truth appear!"

ancient Babylonian prayer, c. 1500 B.C.E.
translated from Sumerian by N. K. Sandars

The Sleep Test

In the beginning, Nzambi slid down to earth on a rainbow,
and there created the animals and the trees. After this he also
created a man and a woman, and he told them to marry and
have children. Nzambi imposed only one prohibition upon
men, that they should not sleep when the moon was up. If
they disobeyed this command, they would be punished with
death. When the first man had become old and had poor eye-
sight, it once happened that the moon was veiled behind the
clouds, so that he could not see it shine. He went to sleep
and died in his sleep. Since then all men have died, because
they are unable to keep awake when the moon is up.

African (Lunda) folktale

Gethsemane

And the day before the Passover and the festival of Unleavened Bread, in the evening, he came into the city with the Twelve, and they ate supper. And after they had sung a psalm, they went out to the Mount of Olives, across the Kidron valley, to a garden called Gethsemane.

And Jesus said, "Sit here, while I pray." And going off by himself, he prostrated himself on the ground and prayed. And he said, "Abba, all things are possible for you. Take this cup from me. Nevertheless, not what I want, but what you want."

And when he got up from his prayer and went to the disciples, he found them asleep. And he said to them, "Why are you sleeping? Couldn't you stay awake for even one hour?" And they didn't know what to answer.

retold by Stephen Mitchell

Drinking Alone by Moonlight

A cup of wine, under the flowering trees;
I drink alone, for no friend is near.
Raising my cup I beckon the bright moon,
For he, with my shadow, will make three men.
The moon, alas, is no drinker of wine;

Listless, my shadow creeps about at my side.
Yet with the moon as friend and the shadow as slave
I must make merry before the Spring is spent.
To the songs I sing the moon flickers her beams;
In the dance I weave my shadow tangles and breaks.
While we were sober, three shared the fun;
Now we are drunk, each goes his way.
May we long share our odd, inanimate feast,
And meet at last on the Cloudy River of the sky.

Li Po, 701–762
translated from Chinese by Arthur Waley

◐

A Medieval Jewish Prayer

Lord, let Your light be only for the day,
And the darkness for the night.
And let my dress, my poor humble dress
Lie quietly over my chair at night.

Let the church-bells be silent,
My neighbour Ivan not ring them at night.
Let the wind not waken the children
Out of their sleep at night.

Let the hen sleep on its roost, the horse in the stable
All through the night.

Remove the stone from the middle of the road
That the thief may not stumble at night.

Let heaven be quiet during the night,
Restrain the lightning, silence the thunder,
They should not frighten mothers giving birth
To their babies at night.

And me too protect against fire and water,
Protect my poor roof at night.
Let my dress, my poor humble dress
Lie quietly over my chair at night.

Nechum Bronze

On the Beach at Night

On the beach at night,
Stands a child with her father,
Watching the east, the autumn sky.

Up through the darkness,
While ravening clouds, the burial clouds, in black masses
     spreading,
Lower sullen and fast athwart and down the sky,
Amid a transparent clear belt of ether yet left in the east,
Ascends large and calm the lord-star Jupiter,

And nigh at hand, only a very little above,
Swim the delicate sisters the Pleiades.

From the beach the child holding the hand of her father,
Those burial-clouds that lower victorious soon to devour all,
Watching, silently weeps.

Weep not, child,
Weep not, my darling,
With these kisses let me remove your tears,
The ravening clouds shall not long be victorious,
They shall not long possess the sky, they devour the stars
    only in apparition,
Jupiter shall emerge, be patient, watch again another night,
    the Pleiades shall emerge,
They are immortal, all those stars both silvery and golden
    shall shine out again,
The great stars and the little ones shall shine out again, they
    endure,
The vast immortal suns and the long-enduring pensive
    moons shall again shine.

Then dearest child mournest thou only for Jupiter?
Considerest thou alone the burial of the stars?

Something there is,
(With my lips soothing thee, adding I whisper,
I give thee the first suggestion, the problem and indirection,)

Something there is more immortal even than the stars,
(Many the burials, many the days and nights, passing away,)
Something that shall endure longer even than lustrous
    Jupiter,
Longer than sun or any revolving satellite,
Or the radiant sisters the Pleiades.

      Walt Whitman, 1819–1892

◐

Each Breath of Night

Like any out-of-the-way-place, the Napo River in the
Ecuadorian jungle seems real enough when you are there,
even central. Out of the way of *what*? I was sitting on a
stump at the edge of a bankside palm-thatch village, in the
middle of the night, on the headwaters of the Amazon.
Out of the way of human life, tenderness, or the glance
of heaven?

    A nightjar in deep-leaved shadow called three long
notes, and hushed. The men with me talked softly in
clumps: three North Americans, four Ecuadorians who
were showing us the jungle. We were holding cool drinks
and idly watching a hand-sized tarantula seize moths that
came to the lone bulb on the generator shed beside us.

It was February, the middle of summer. Green fireflies spattered lights across the air and illumined for seconds, now here, now there, the pale trunks of enormous, solitary trees. Beneath us the brown Napo River was rising, in all silence; it coiled up the sandy bank and tangled its foam in vines that trailed from the forest and roots that looped the shore.

Each breath of night smelled sweet, more moistened and sweet than any kitchen, or garden, or cradle. Each star in Orion seemed to tremble and stir with my breath. All at once, in the thatch house across the clearing behind us, one of the village's Jesuit priests began playing an alto recorder, playing a wordless song, lyric, in a minor key, that twined over the village clearing, that caught in the big trees' canopies, muted our talk on the bankside, and wandered over the river, dissolving downstream.

This will do, I thought. This will do, for a weekend, or a season, or a home.

Annie Dillard

◑

Acquainted with the Night

I have been one acquainted with the night.
I have walked out in rain—and back in rain.
I have outwalked the furthest city light.

I have looked down the saddest city lane.
I have passed by the watchman on his beat
And dropped my eyes, unwilling to explain.

I have stood still and stopped the sound of feet
When far away an interrupted cry
Came over houses from another street,

But not to call me back or say good-bye;
And further still at an unearthly height,
One luminary clock against the sky

Proclaimed the time was neither wrong nor right.
I have been one acquainted with the night.

Robert Frost, 1874–1963

The Heart of Herakles

Lying under the stars,
In the summer night,
Late, while the autumn
Constellations climb the sky,
As the Cluster of Hercules
Falls down the west
I put the telescope by
And watch Deneb
Move towards the zenith.

My body is asleep. Only
My eyes and brain are awake.
The stars stand around me
Like gold eyes. I can no longer
Tell where I begin and leave off.
The faint breeze in the dark pines,
And the invisible grass,
The tipping earth, the swarming stars
Have an eye that sees itself.

Kenneth Rexroth, 1905–1982

Glaciers by Starlight

We gathered a lot of fossil wood and after supper made a
big fire, and as we sat around it the brightness of the sky
brought on a long talk with the Indians about the stars; and
their eager, childlike attention was refreshing to see as com-
pared with the deathlike apathy of weary town-dwellers, in
whom natural curiosity has been quenched in toil and care
and poor shallow comfort.

After sleeping a few hours, I stole quietly out of the
camp, and climbed the mountain that stands between the
two glaciers. The ground was frozen, making the climbing
difficult in the steepest places; but the views over the icy

bay, sparkling beneath the stars, were enchanting. It seemed then a sad thing that any part of so precious a night had been lost in sleep. The starlight was so full that I distinctly saw not only the berg-filled bay, but most of the lower portions of the glaciers, lying pale and spirit-like amid the mountains. The nearest glacier in particular was so distinct that it seemed to be glowing with light that came from within itself. Not even in dark nights have I ever found any difficulty in seeing large glaciers; but on this mountain-top, amid so much ice, in the heart of so clear and frosty a night, everything was more or less luminous, and I seemed to be poised in a vast hollow between two skies of almost equal brightness. This exhilarating scramble made me glad and strong and I rejoiced that my studies called me before the glorious night succeeding so glorious a morning had been spent!

John Muir, 1838–1914

Alone in the Arctic Night

April 22, 1934

. . . It is now close to midnight. In a moment I shall go to bed. I know exactly what I shall do. With a pencil stroke, I shall cross this day off the calendar; then fetch snow and alcohol tablets for the morning tea, and, finally, make sure that the instruments are functioning properly. This inspection over, I shall take a quick glance from the hatch to see whether anything unusual is happening in the auroral department. After battening down the trapdoor, I shall undress, turn down the pressure lantern, put out the fire, open the door, and jump for the sleeping bag, leaving the storm lantern burning over my head. That part of the routine is automatic. As long as heat remains in the shack, I shall read; tonight it will be the second volume of the *Life of Alexander,* which I've nearly finished. That part is by choice. When my hands turn numb, I'll reach up and blow out the lantern, but not until I have first made sure that the flashlight is somewhere in the sleeping bag, where my body will keep the battery warm.

I don't try to force myself to sleep, as I sometimes do at home. My whole life here in a sense is an experiment in harmony, and I let the bodily processes achieve a natural equilibrium. As a rule, it doesn't take me long to go to sleep. But a man can live a lifetime in a few half-dreaming moments of introspection between going to bed and falling asleep: a lifetime reordered and edited to satisfy the ever-changing demands of the mind.

Richard E. Byrd, 1888–1957

Night Flight

You can live a lifetime and, at the end of it, know more about other people than you know about yourself. You learn to watch other people, but you never watch yourself because you strive against loneliness. If you read a book, or shuffle a deck of cards, or care for a dog, you are avoiding yourself. The abhorrence of loneliness is as natural as wanting to live at all. If it were otherwise, men would never have bothered to make an alphabet, nor to have fashioned words out of what were only animal sounds, nor to have crossed continents—each man to see what the other looked like.

Being alone in an aeroplane for even so short a time as a night and a day, irrevocably alone, with nothing to observe but your instruments and your own hands in semi-darkness, nothing to contemplate but the size of your small courage, nothing to wonder about but the beliefs, the faces, and the hopes rooted in your mind—such an experience can be as startling as the first awareness of a stranger walking by your side at night. You are the stranger.

It is dark already and I am over the south of Ireland. There are the lights of Cork and the lights are wet; they are drenched in Irish rain, and I am above them and dry. I am above them and the plane roars in a sobbing world, but it imparts no sadness to me. I feel the security of solitude, the exhilaration of escape. So long as I can see the lights and imagine the people walking under them, I feel selfishly triumphant, as if I have eluded care and left even the small sorrow of rain in other hands.

It is a little over an hour now since I left Abingdon. England, Wales, and the Irish Sea are behind me like so much time used up. On a long flight distance and time are the same. But there had been a moment when Time stopped—and Distance too. It was the moment I lifted the blue-and-silver Gull from the aerodrome, the moment the photographers aimed their cameras, the moment I felt the craft refuse its burden and strain toward the earth in sullen rebellion, only to listen at last to the persuasion of stick and elevators, the dogmatic argument of blueprints that said she *had* to fly because the figures proved it.

So she had flown, and once airborne, once she had yielded to the sophistry of a draughtsman's board, she had said, "There: I have lifted the weight. Now, where are we bound?"—and the question had frightened me.

"We are bound for a place thirty-six hundred miles from here—two thousand miles of it unbroken ocean. Most of the way it will be night. We are flying west with the night."

Beryl Markham, 1902–1986

You Darkness, That I Come From

You darkness, that I come from,
I love you more than all the fires
that fence in the world,
for the fire makes
a circle of light for everyone,
and then no one outside learns of you.

But the darkness pulls in everything:
shapes and fires, animals and myself,
how easily it gathers them!—
powers and people—

and it is possible a great energy
is moving near me.

I have faith in nights.

Rainer Maria Rilke, 1875–1926
translated from German by Robert Bly

Rhyming in the Darkness

This is the world I love best—the world lit by starlight.
There are a few dozen electric lights burning in the parish
below me, and I can make out another dozen or so lights on

the Iveragh Peninsula across Dingle Bay, including the resolute beacon of the Valentia Harbour lighthouse. My immediate environment—the grassy bank, the hedge of honeysuckle and fuchsia, the wild irises and foxgloves massed in the ditch—is illuminated solely by the light of stars. Vega, at the zenith, is a thousand times less bright than the full moon, fifty million times less bright than the sun. But multiply Vega's faint light by the 10,000 stars of the summer Milky Way, and it is illumination enough.

In the bardic schools of ancient Ireland, the young poets-in-training, having been set in the evening a theme for composition, retired each one to his private cell, a cell furnished with nothing more than a bed and perhaps a peg on which to hang a cloak, and—most importantly—without windows, there to compose the requisite rhymes, taking care to observe the designated rules as to syllables, quartans, concord, correspondence, termination, and union, in *total darkness,* throughout the remainder of the night and all the next day, undistracted by the least ray of the sun, until the following evening at an appointed time when a light was brought in and the poem written down. An eighteenth-century account of the bardic schools by the Marquis of Claricarde asserts that the discipline of darkness was imposed so that the young poets might avoid the "Distractions which Light and the variety of Objects represented thereby commonly occasions," and in darkness "more fully focus the Faculties of the Soul" upon the subject at hand. From the Marquis' language one might suppose that the soul has a light of its own, that it glows with a self-luminosity, like the owls of the Blackwater Valley, and that the soul's crepuscular light is drowned out by the light of day. Certainly poets, like mystics, have traditionally been creatures of the night. The world of daylight is a world of impenetrable surfaces, resplendent, metallic, adamantine. In starlight, surfaces are transparent, like the flesh of a hand held to a bright light, and the soul sees into objects and beyond. But there is a danger in starlight—the danger of infinite dilution. There is a danger that the soul will leak away like water into loose soil, or be dispersed like breath in wind. Could that be why the poets of the bardic schools shut themselves up in *total* darkness to compose their verses, without the light of a single star? The light of one star is enough to prick night's dark skin, and the enclosing sphere of the sky goes pop like a balloon, and we fall out of ourselves, upward, toward Vega, at twelve miles per second, into Infinity.

Chet Raymo

El Greco's Parable of Genius

I walk by myself
at night, in the dark.
Someone lights a candle
in the distance.

In his country house
he burns the wick
that hardly illuminates
the depth of his room.

In the twilight moves
the master of the candle,
its flickering flame
is little more than nothing.

But to the wanderer
it is a guiding signal,
to be seen miles away
in the blind night.

Its flicker marks
the direction of my village
like a huge bonfire
across the night.

> *Sándor Weöres*
> translated from Hungarian by William Jay Smith

●

Piano Man

Friday night. Beautiful jazz piano at Picante's. Two people in
the room. Three grubby skateboarders and several ticket
holders waiting for their food in the next. The music, simple,

yet impossibly lovely, impossibly complicated, pours out of the shiny black spinet. The piano player notices me listening. He can hear me listening. He turns his head slightly to look. I look away to avoid eye contact because the music is impossibly intimate. How can I tell him that it's okay that no one but me hears? That I will walk out and down Sixth Street and he will be alone but that he must not stop playing? That he is not alone as long as he sounds? That he means as long as he sounds? That he cannot stop playing. He must not.

Joyce Jenkins

Childfoot Visitation

One night traveling a Green Tortoise bus
    San Francisco to Seattle,
The rear of the bus converted to pads for sleeping,
Sleeping on my back as we plunged through pouring rain,
    the other weary passengers sleeping,
Suddenly something moving in my beard and under my nose
    woke me up—
Opening my eyes in the darkness
    I saw in the flickering headlight patterns
    of passing cars

The small foot of the little girl sleeping
    beside her mother.
Cleansmelling childfoot flower stretching beneath my nose
    as she changed position in her dream.
Gently pushing it away, careful not to wake her,
    I drifted off to sleep
Thinking how many men who never had a child
    are visited by a childhood foot
    slowly sliding through their beards
    opening their eyes to
    its perfect shape in the twilight?
Suddenly out of Eternity coming to me
    white and pink and smelling good,
For the first time in my life
    a little girl's naked foot
    woke me up.

      Antler

◑

Runaway

There are sparkles of rain on the bright
Hair over your forehead;
Your eyes are wet and your lips
Wet and cold, your cheek rigid with cold.

Why have you stayed
Away so long, why have you only
Come to me late at night
After walking for hours in wind and rain?
Take off your dress and stockings;
Sit in the deep chair before the fire.
I will warm your feet in my hands;
I will warm your breasts and thighs with kisses.
I wish I could build a fire
In you that would never go out.
I wish I could be sure that deep in you
Was a magnet to draw you always home.

Kenneth Rexroth, 1905–1982

Ballad of the Dogs

When Ibn Batutta, Arabian traveler,
physician, clear-eyed observer of the world,
born in Maghreb in the fourteenth century, came
to the city of Bulgar, he learnt about the Darkness.
This "Darkness" was a country, forty days' travel
further to the north. At the end of Ramadan,
when he broke his fast at sunset, he had barely time
to intone the night prayer before day

broke again. The birches glimmered whitely.
Ibn Batutta, Arabian traveler, journeyed
no further north than Bulgar. But the tales he heard
of the Darkness, and of the visits there, engrossed him.
This journey is made only by rich merchants,
who take hundreds of sledges with them, loaded
with food, drink and firewood, for the ground there
is covered with ice and no one can keep his balance.
Except the dogs: their claws take firm hold
of the eternal ice. No trees, no stones,
no huts can serve the traveler as landmarks.
Only those long-lived dogs are guides into
the Country of the Darkness, those old dogs
who have made the journey many times before.
They can cost a thousand dinars, or even more,
since for their knowledge there is no substitute.
At meals they are always served before the men:
otherwise the leading dog grows angry
and escapes, leaving its master to his fate.
In the great Darkness. After they have traveled
for forty days the merchants make a halt,
place their wares on the ground and return to their camp.
Returning on the following day they find
heaps of sable, ermine, miniver,
set down a little apart from their own pile.
If the merchant is content with this exchange
he takes the skins. If not, he leaves them there.

Then the inhabitants of the Darkness raise
their bid with more furs, or else take back
everything they laid out before, rejecting
the foreigners' goods. Such is the way they trade.
Ibn Batutta returned to Maghreb, and there
at a great age he died. But these dogs,
mute but sagacious, lacking the power of speech
and yet with a blind certainty that guides them
across wind-polished ice into the Darkness,
will never leave us in peace.
We speak, and what we say knows more than we do.
We think, and what we thought runs on before us,
as if that thought knew something we didn't know.
Messages travel through history, a code
masquerading as ideas
but meant for someone other than ourselves.
The history of ideas is not a knowledge of the mind.
And the dogs go on, with sure and swishing steps,
deeper into the Darkness.

Lars Gustafsson
translated from Swedish by Philip Martin

The Dark Night of the Soul

For some, night is a blessing, for others, a haunting. The dark powers that inspire can also conspire. The English poet A. E. Housman captured the corrosive difference when he wrote in "A Shropshire Lad," "And fire and ice within me fight / Beneath the suffocating night." In a room where we can't breathe, dreams are transmogrified; hope disintegrates into despair; faith corrodes into cynicism. Night is no longer friend but foe. "Ain't it just like the night," moans the old blues singer, "to play tricks when you're trying to be quiet?"

Not so many generations ago, it was ardently believed that an oppressive feeling during sleep was caused by something sitting on one's chest. The *grimoires* of the time were full of spells to fight off the monster variously called a night-hag, a *cauchemar,* "the fiend that tramples," a wild horse, a demented mare. Hence, the nemesis word *nightmare,* which haunts this sleepstrange part of the book. Out of the sheer cussedness of insomniac nights roiling with bad dreams come the melancholic, anguished words of souls who haven't got a prayer and find night a torture chamber, the bed a rack, and sleep a canvas of Magritte phantoms.

Call it the time of shadowboxing. For lovers like Ovid, during sleepless nights "cruel love torments the breast." For Samuel

Coleridge, the dark night is a bout with a "fiendish dream," and for James Joyce, night brings "a riot of emotions." In the double-fisted words of Dylan Thomas, "Rage, rage against the dying of the light." These are the stalking hours of vampires, "silhouettes" to poet Diane Ackerman, who silkenly asks to be "jolted" so she might earn her own night wings.

And yet, apparently more can come of sleep problems than apparitions. During the early eighteenth century, a certain Count Goldberg, the slumberless Russian ambassador to Germany approached the greatest composer of the era with a curious request in the form of a commission. Johann Sebastian Bach's *Goldberg Variations* were the answer, a musical cure for the diplomat's insomnia. The record does not show, however, if the Count slept the night he first heard the music. A rhapsody on the theme comes from the late nineteenth century in England. If an insomnolent ambassador had gone to Lewis Carroll, he would probably have been given a set of math problems, "calming calculations," from the fantisist's *Bedside Book,* remedies for the "harrassing thoughts that are apt to invade a wholly-unoccupied mind."

These cameos about creative responses to sleep deprivation anticipate several writers in this part. "Night Rain," by Izumi Shikibu, is a triumph of creative melancholy or healing wistfulness over the paralysis of insomnia, which was rampant in the imperial courts of Kyoto a thousand years ago. In a passage from *The Night Country,* naturalist Loren Eiseley writes of his "midnight examinations," confessing that he avoided his own bedroom door because it resembled "the gateway to the tomb." After quoting Shakespeare on how the mad world "does murder sleep," Eiseley reveals how his grandmother finally led him "out of a dark room and retied [his] thread of life to the living world." In "The Man on the Hotel Room Bed," Galway Kinnell limns the lonely anticipation in drafty hotel rooms, where the lone traveler is waiting and hoping to be swaddled in the "arms of prayer."

Finally, for those not convinced by Anthony Burgess that "there is no cure for nocturnal horrors except not going to bed," there is movie therapy. *The Cure for Insomnia* is not the life story of Goldberg, the Russian ambassador, or the name of a snake oil salesman's brochure. Instead, it's the title of the longest film on record, a strategically soporific eighty-seven-hour-long documentary.

Say no more; some of us come from rusted nights.

Insomnia

When the bird of sleep
thought to nest
in my eye

it saw the eyelashes
and flew away
for fear of nets.

Abū ʿĀmir ibn al-Hammārah, 12th century
translated by Cola Franzen
from the Spanish versions of Emilio García Gómez

All Night I Could Not Sleep

All night I could not sleep
Because of the moonlight on my bed
I kept on hearing a voice calling:
Out of Nowhere, Nothing answered, "yes."

Zi Ye, 6th–3rd century B.C.E.
translated from Chinese by Arthur Waley

Winter Night

My bed is so empty that I keep on waking up:
As the cold increases, the night-wind begins to blow.
It rustles the curtains, making a noise like the sea:
Oh that those were waves which could carry me back
    to you!

Yang-ti, 605–617
translated from Chinese by Arthur Waley

Untouched by Sleep

What shall I say this means, that my couch seems so hard,
and the coverlets will not stay in place, and I pass the long,

long night, untouched by sleep, and the weary bones of my tossing body are filled with ache?—for I should know, I think, were I in any way assailed by love. Or can it be that love has stolen into me, and cunningly works my harm with covered art? Thus it must be; the subtle darts are planted in my heart, and cruel love torments the breast where he is lord.

Ovid, 43 B.C.E.–17 C.E.
translated from Latin by Christopher Marlowe

Folk Rhyme

Saint Francis and Saint Benedight
Blesse this house from wicked wight,
From the night-mare and the goblin,
That is hight Good-fellow Robin;
Keep it from all evil spirits,
Fairies, weezels, rats and ferrets,
From curfew time
To the next prime.

traditional English

Night Rain

I think, "At least in my dreams
we'll be able to meet . . ."
Moving my pillow
this way and that on the bed,
completely unable to sleep.

You ask my thoughts
through the long night?
I spent it listening
to the heavy rain
beating against the windows.

Izumi Shikibu, 974?–1034?
translated from Japanese by Jane Hirshfield with Mariko Aratani

◑

O Friends, I Am Mad

O friends, I am mad
with love, and no one sees.

My mattress is a sword-point,
how can I sleep
when the bed of my Beloved
is spread open elsewhere?

Only those who have felt the knife
can understand the wound,
only the jeweler
knows the nature of the Jewel.

I have lost it,
and though anguish takes me door to door,
no doctor answers.

Mira calls her Lord: O Dark One,
Only You can heal this pain.

Mirabai, 1498–1565?
translated from medieval Hindi by Jane Hirshfield

The Pains of Sleep

Ere on my bed my limbs I lay,
It hath not been my use to pray
With moving lips or bended knees;
But silently, by slow degrees,
My spirit I to Love compose,
In humble trust mine eye-lids close,
With reverential resignation,
No wish conceived, no thought exprest,
Only a sense of supplication;
A sense o'er all my soul imprest

That I am weak, yet not unblest,
Since in me, round me, every where
Eternal Strength and Wisdom are.

But yester-night I prayed aloud
In anguish and in agony,
Up-starting from the fiendish crowd
Of shapes and thoughts that tortured me:
A lurid light, a trampling throng,
Sense of intolerable wrong,
And whom I scorned, those only strong!
Thirst of revenge, the powerless will
Still baffled, and yet burning still!
Desire with loathing strangely mixed
On wild or hateful objects fixed.
Fantastic passions! maddening brawl!
And shame and terror over all!
Deeds to be hid which were not hid,
Which all confused I could not know
Whether I suffered, or I did:
For all seemed guilt, remorse or woe,
My own or others' still the same
Life-stifling fear, soul-stifling shame.

So two nights passed: the night's dismay
Saddened and stunned the coming day.
Sleep, the wide blessing, seemed to me
Distemper's worst calamity.

The third night, when my own loud scream
Had waked me from the fiendish dream,
O'ercome with sufferings strange and wild,
I wept as I had been a child;
And having thus by tears subdued
My anguish to a milder mood,
Such punishments, I said, were due
To natures deepliest stained with sin,—
For aye entempesting anew
The unfathomable hell within,
The horror of their deeds to view,
To know and loathe, yet wish and do!
Such griefs with such men well agree,
But wherefore, wherefore fall on me?
To be beloved is all I need,
And whom I love, I love indeed.

Samuel Coleridge, 1772–1834

from "The Dead"

She was fast asleep.

Gabriel, leaning on his elbow, looked for a few
moments unresentfully on her tangled hair and half-open
mouth, listening to her deep-drawn breath. So she had had
that romance in her life: a man had died for her sake. It

hardly pained him now to think how poor a part he, her husband, had played in her life. He watched her while she slept, as though he and she had never lived together as man and wife. His curious eyes rested long upon her face and on her hair; and as he thought of what she must have been then, in that time of her first girlish beauty, a strange, friendly pity for her entered his soul. He did not like to say even to himself that her face was no longer beautiful, but he knew that it was no longer the face for which Michael Furey had braved death.

Perhaps she had not told him all the story. His eyes moved to the chair over which she had thrown some of her clothes. A petticoat string dangled to the floor. One boot stood upright, its limp upper fallen down: the fellow of it lay upon its side. He wondered at his riot of emotions of an hour before. From what had it proceeded? From his aunt's supper, from his own foolish speech, from the wine and dancing, the merry-making when saying good night in the hall, the pleasure of the walk along the river in the snow. Poor Aunt Julia! She, too, would soon be a shade with the shade of Patrick Morkan and his horse. He had caught that haggard look upon her face for a moment when she was singing *Arrayed for the Bridal.* Soon, perhaps, he would be sitting in that same drawing-room, dressed in black, his silk hat on his knees. The blinds would be drawn down and Aunt Kate would be sitting beside him, crying and blowing her

nose and telling him how Julia had died. He would cast
about in his mind for some words that might console her,
and would find only lame and useless ones. Yes, yes: that
would happen very soon.

The air of the room chilled his shoulders. He stretched
himself cautiously along under the sheets and lay down
beside his wife. One by one, they were all becoming shades.
Better pass boldly into that other world, in the full glory of
some passion, than fade and wither dismally with age. He
thought of how she who lay beside him had locked in her
heart for so many years that image of her lover's eyes when
he had told her that he did not wish to live.

Generous tears filled Gabriel's eyes. He had never felt
that himself towards any woman, but he knew that such a
feeling must be love. The tears gathered more thickly in his
eyes and in the partial darkness he imagined he saw the
form of a young man standing under a dripping tree. Other
forms were near. His soul had approached that region where
dwell the vast hosts of the dead. He was conscious of, but
could not apprehend, their wayward and flickering exis-
tence. His own identity was fading out into a grey impalpa-
ble world: the solid world itself, which these dead had one
time reared and lived in, was dissolving and dwindling.

A few light taps upon the pane made him turn to the
window. It had begun to snow again. He watched sleepily
the flakes, silver and dark, falling obliquely against the

lamplight. The time had come for him to set out on his journey westwards. Yes, the newspapers were right: snow was general all over Ireland. It was falling on every part of the dark central plain, on the treeless hills, falling softly upon the Bog of Allen and, further westwards, softly falling into the dark mutinous Shannon waves. It was falling, too, upon every part of the lonely churchyard on the hill where Michael Furey lay buried. It lay thickly drifted on the crooked crosses and headstones, on the spears of the little gate, on the barren thorns. His soul swooned slowly as he heard the snow falling faintly through the universe and faintly falling, like the descent of their last end, upon all the living and the dead.

James Joyce, 1882–1941

●

One Night's Dying

There is always a soft radiance beyond the bedroom door from a night-light behind my chair. I have lived this way for many years now. I sleep or I do not sleep, and the light makes no difference except if I wake. Then, as I awaken, the dim forms of objects sustain my grip on reality. The familiar chair, the walls of the book-lined study reassert my own existence.

I do not lie and toss with doubt any longer, as I did in earlier years. I get up and write, as I am writing now, or I read in the old chair that is as worn as I am. I read philosophy, metaphysics, difficult works that sometime, soon or late, draw a veil over my eyes so that I drowse in my chair.

It is not that I fail to learn from these midnight examinations of the world. It is merely that I choose that examination to remain as remote and abstruse as possible. Even so, I cannot always prophesy the result. An obscure line may whirl me into a wide-awake, ferocious concentration in which ideas like animals leap at me out of the dark, in which sudden odd trains of thought drive me inexorably to my desk and paper. I am, in short, a victim of insomnia—sporadic, wearing, violent, and melancholic. In the words of Shakespeare, for the world "does murder sleep." It has been so since my twentieth year.

In that year my father died—a man well loved, the mainstay of our small afflicted family. He died slowly in severe bodily torture. My mother was stone-deaf. I, his son, saw and heard him die. We lived in a place and time not free with the pain-alleviating drugs of later decades. When the episode of many weeks' duration was over, a curious thing happened: I could no longer bear the ticking of the alarm clock in my own bedroom.

At first I smothered it with an extra blanket in a box beside my cot, but the ticking persisted as though it came from my own head. I used to lie for hours staring into the dark of the sleeping house, feeling the loneliness that only the sleepless know when the queer feeling comes that it is the sleeping who are alive and those awake are disembodied ghosts. Finally, in desperation, I gave up the attempt to sleep and turned to reading, though it was difficult to concentrate.

It was then that human help appeared. My grandmother saw the light burning through the curtains of my door and came to sit with me. A few years later, when I touched her hair in farewell at the beginning of a journey from which I would not return to see her alive, I knew she had saved my sanity. Into that lonely room at midnight she had come, abandoning her own sleep, in order to sit with one in trouble. We had not talked much, but we had sat together by the lamp, reasserting our common humanity before the great empty dark that is the universe.

Grandmother knew nothing of psychiatry. She had not reestablished my sleep patterns, but she had done something more important. She had brought me out of a dark room and retied my thread of life to the living world. Henceforward, by night or day, though I have been subject to the moods of depression or gaiety which are a part of the lives of all of us, I have been able not merely to endure but to make the best of what many regard as an unbearable affliction.

It is true that as an educational administrator I can occasionally be caught nodding in lengthy committee meetings, but so, I have observed, can men who come from sound nights on their pillows. Strangely, I, who frequently grow round-eyed and alert as an owl at the stroke of midnight, find it pleasant to nap in daylight among friends. I can roll up on a couch and sleep peacefully while my wife and chatting friends who know my peculiarities keep the daytime universe safely under control. Or so it seems. For, deep-seated in my subconscious, is perhaps the idea that the black bedroom door is the gateway to the tomb.

I try in that bedroom to sleep high on two pillows, to have ears and eyes alert. Something shadowy has to be held in place and controlled. At night one has to sustain reality without help. One has to hear lest hearing be lost, see lest sight not return to follow moonbeams across the floor, touch lest the sense of objects vanish. Oh, sleeping, soundlessly sleeping ones, do you ever think who knits your universe together safely from one day's memory to the next? It is the insomniac, not the night policeman on his beat.

Many will challenge this point of view. They will say that electric power does the trick, that many a roisterer stumbles down the long street at dawn, after having served his purpose of holding the links of the mad world together. There are parts of the nighttime world, men say to me, that it is just as well I do not know. Go home and sleep, man. Others will keep your giddy world together. Let the thief pass quickly in the shadow, he is awake. Let the juvenile gangs which sidle like bands of evil crabs up from the dark waters of poverty into prosperous streets pass without finding you at midnight.

The advice is good, but in the city or the country small things important to our lives have no reporter except as he who does not sleep may observe them. And that man must be disencumbered of reality. He must have no commitments to the dark, as do the murderer and thief. Only he must see, though what he sees may come from the night side of the planet that no man knows well. For even in the early dawn, while men lie unstirring in their sleep or stumble sleepy-eyed to work, some single episode may turn the whole world for a moment into the place of marvel that it is, but that we grow too day-worn to accept.

Loren Eiseley, 1907–1977

◐

Rosary

Here is a man walking on a road under the half-moon. The trees are tall and well-furred; the light is little. In his left hand, sometimes swinging at his side and sometimes held lightly poised over his heart, he counts the crystal beads of a rosary. After a quarter of a mile of dark road, he passes a large building of some hard to determine kind. In a ground floor wing, one room is brightly lit; near a window sits a woman with glossy black hair, bent to some papers. The man admires the profile, the hair, the air of industriousness. He likes people who work hard. He walks on, dismissing the notion of rapping on window or door and chatting with the woman. It must be frightening to be a woman alone in a building at night, when the building itself is alone in the countryside, nothing for half a mile round except trees and a man with crystal beads in his hand and the young deer he had seen cross the road in front of him a few minutes back. She would be scared if I knocked, he thought, and walked on.

Now it may be that before the man had drawn abreast of the window the woman had seen him coming, had looked out casually from a darkened window in another room and seen this man stepping up the intermittently moonlit road. It may be that the gleam of crystal in his hand seemed to her the gleam of moon on dagger. It may be that she longed for this silent shadowy assassin to come destroy her, to rescue her from hard work or loneliness or her glossy hair. It may be that she posed at the lighted window to woo his attention, and long after he passed still hoped he might be lurking in the rhododendrons. Perhaps ten minutes later she bravely, desperately stepped out of the unbolted door and stood on the lawn and saw no one but the same deer browsing under the fruit trees. Or not the same: who can tell one animal from another?

Robert Kelly

Seven Nocturnals

I

Dream after dream arrived
For the jasmine's birthday,
Night after night for the white insomnia
Of the swans

Coolness is born among leaves
As is the starlit sensation
In boundless sky.

II

Propitious starlight brought on silence
And behind the silence an intrusive melody
Lover,
Temptress of sounds from another country.

Now the dying shadow remains
And its cracked confidence,
Its incurable dizziness—there.

III

All the cypress trees point toward midnight
All the fingers
Toward silence

Outside the dream's open window
Slowly, slowly

The confession unwinds
And, as pure colour, deviates toward the stars!

IV

A shoulder fully bared
Like truth
Pays for its precision
At this edge of evening
Which shines in isolation
Under the secret half-moon
Of my nostalgia.

V

Unguarded night was taken by memories
Dark blue
Red
Yellow

Its open arms filled with sleep
Its rested hair with wind
Its eyes with silence.

VI

Unfathomable night, bitterness without limit
Sleepless eyelash
Pain burns before it turns to sobbing
Loss leans off-balance before its weighing

Ambush at the point of death
When thought is broken by the useless meandering design
On the apron of its destiny.

VII

The moon's diadem on the brow of night
When shadows divide up the surface
Of vision

And pain measured by the practised ear
Unintentionally collapses
Inside an idea made worthless by the melancholy
Of evening's bugle-call.

> *Odysseus Elytis*
> translated from Greek by Edmund Keeley and Philip Sherrard

●

Lines to a Granny*

Granny,
tell me again in the dark
about the wandering prince;
and his steed, with a neem-leaf mark
upon his brow, will prance
again to splash his noonday image

* Who told me the story of "The Sleeping Beauty"

in the sleep of these pools. He will break
with sesame words
known only to the birds,
the cobweb curtained door; and wake
the sentinel, the bawdy cook;
the parrot in the cage
will shout his name
to the gossip of the kitchen's blowzy flame.

Let him, dear granny,
shape the darkness
and take again
the princess
whose breath would hardly strain
the spider's design.

But tell me now: was it for some irony
you have waited in death
to let me learn again what once you learnt in youth,
that this is no tale, but truth?

A. K. Ramanujan

Silhouette

Nightwing, you live in coffins
by day, a mortuary scribe

writing ads for guilt
abstract as leached bone,
with words like "perpetual,"
"always," and "everlasting,"
words too mineral
to use whole with a lover.
To feed your art,
you sell bereavement and brass.
But by night you fly.
Blood draws you out.
Your luxuriant fur glistens
in moonlight, as you steal women's souls.
Earthbound, they come
to sup with you in mid-air,
to give up reflection,
to learn to travel light,
as you roam the quiet spirals
of the world, squashing blossoms
against their pale necks.

Tonight, the air's a cool, slick whisper
to be flown, a benediction
of damp. Everything is at stake.
But all my pelts are twitching tight.
Already moths are beating
in my veins. Love, come drive

your purple fangs in steep,
and jolt me from my flesh tonight,
let me earn my wings.

Dianne Ackerman

Do Not Go Gentle into That Good Night

Do not go gentle into that good night,
Old age should burn and rave at close of day;
Rage, rage against the dying of the light.

Though wise men at their end know dark is right,
Because their words had forked no lightning they
Do not go gentle into that good night.

Good men, the last wave by, crying how bright
Their frail deeds might have danced in a green bay,
Rage, rage against the dying of the light.

Wild men who caught and sang the sun in flight,
And learn, too late, they grieved it on its way,
Do not go gentle into that good night.

Grave men, near death, who see with blinding sight
Blind eyes could blaze like meteors and be gay,
Rage, rage against the dying of the light.

And you, my father, there on the sad height,
Curse, bless, me now with your fierce tears, I pray.
Do not go gentle into that good night.
Rage, rage against the dying of the light.

Dylan Thomas, 1914–1953

Lying Awake

September 18th

. . . This morning I woke at four and lay awake for an hour
or so in a bad state. It is raining again. I got up finally and
went about the daily chores, waiting for the sense of doom
to lift—and what did it was watering the house plants. Sud-
denly joy came back because I was fulfilling a simple need,
a living one. Dusting never has this effect (and that may be
why I am such a poor housekeeper!), but feeding the cats
when they are hungry, giving Punch clean water, makes me
suddenly feel calm and happy.

Whatever peace I know rests in the natural world, in
feeling myself a part of it, even in a small way. . . . To go
with, not against the elements, an inexhaustible vitality
summoned back each day to do the same tasks, to feed
the animals, clean out barns and pens, keep that complex
world alive.

May Sarton

from Trilce (1922)

XV

In that corner, where we slept together
so many nights, I've sat down now
to take a walk. The bedstead of the dead lovers
has been taken away, or what could have happened.

You came early for other things,
but you're gone now. This is the corner
where I read one night, by your side,
between your tender breasts,
a story by Daudet. It is the corner
we loved. Don't confuse it with any other.

I've started to think about those days
of summer gone, with you entering and leaving,
little and fed up, pale through the rooms.

On this rainy night,
already far from both of us, all at once I jump . . .
There are two doors, swinging open, shut,
two doors in the wind, back, and forth,
shadow   to   shadow.

Cesar Vallejo, 1892–1938
translated from Spanish by James Wright

from Insomnia

Black as the centre of an eye, the centre, a blackness
that sucks at light. I love your vigilance.

Night, first mother of songs, give me the voice to sing of you
in those fingers lies the bridle of the four winds.

Crying out, offering words of homage to you, I am
only a shell where the ocean is still sounding.

But I have looked too long into human eyes
Reduce me now to ashes Night, like a black sun.

Marina Tsvetayeva, 1892–1941
translated from Russian by Elaine Feinstein
and Angela Livingstone

Hotel Insomnia

I liked my little hole,
Its window facing a brick wall.
Next door there was a piano.
A few evenings a month
A crippled old man came to play
"My Blue Heaven."

Mostly, though, it was quiet.
Each room with its spider in heavy overcoat
Catching his fly with a web
Of cigarette smoke and revery.
So dark,
I could not see my face in the shaving mirror.

At 5 A.M. the sound of bare feet upstairs.
The "Gypsy" fortuneteller,
Whose storefront is on the corner,
Going to pee after a night of love.
Once, too, the sound of a child sobbing.
So near it was, I thought
For a moment, I was sobbing myself.

Charles Simic

The Man on the Hotel Room Bed

He shifts on the bed carefully, so as
not to press through the first layer
into the second, which is permanently sore.
For him sleep means lying as still as possible
for as long as possible thinking the worst.

Nor does it help to outlast the night—
in seconds after the light comes
the inner darkness falls over everything.
He wonders if the left hand of the woman
in the print hanging in the dark above the bed,
who sits half turned away, her right hand
clutching her face, lies empty,
or does it move in the hair of a man
who dies, or perhaps died long ago
and sometimes comes and puts his head in her lap,
and then goes back and lies under a sign
in a field filled nearly up to the roots
holding down the hardly ever trampled grass
with mortals, the once-lovers. He goes over
the mathematics of lying awake all night alone
in a strange room: still the equations require
multiplication, by fear, of what is,
to the power of desire. He feels around—
no pillow next to his, no depression
in the pillow, no head in the depression.
Love is the religion that bereaves the bereft.
No doubt his mother's arms still waver up
somewhere reaching for him; and perhaps
his father's are now ready to gather him
there where peace and death dangerously mingle.
But the arms of prayer, which pressed his chest

in childhood—long ago, he himself, in the name
of truth, let them go slack. He lies facedown,
like something washed up. Out the window
first light pinks the glass hotel across
the street. In the religion of love to pray
is to pass, by a shining word, into the inner chamber
of the other. It is to ask the father and mother
to return and be forgiven. But in this religion
not everyone can pray—least of all
a man lying alone to avoid being abandoned,
who wants to die to escape the meeting with death.
The final second strikes. On the glass wall
the daylight grows so bright the man sees
the next darkness already forming inside it.

Galway Kinnell

Reconciling with the Night

"What can we gain by sailing to the moon," Thomas Merton asked in his book *Thoughts in Solitude,* "if we are not able to cross the abyss that separates us from ourselves?" Longing, grieving, and yearning, according to the sages, are but stages on the journey. Eventually we must find a way to endure, to move across, to vanquish sorrows, apply salve to wounds that they may heal into scars. In "June Intercedes in the Garden of Roses," Elizabeth Macklin asks,

> Was it the fear of loss
> that kept you awake last night?
>
> There's no hurry, no hurry, today.

What *did* keep us awake? What kept us afraid for so long? Can we "hold on in the darkness," as the poet exhorts? Can we kneel in the dark long enough, as my Gramma Dora used to urge, until we see the light? *What can we salvage from the night?*

The selections in this part mark the still point of the night journey. D. H. Lawrence, the man who once said the world gave him "the gruesomes," reveals his trust in the night's galvanic moments when he asks in "Song of a Man Who Has Come Through":

What is the knocking at the door in the night?
It is somebody wants to do us harm.

No, no, it is the three strange angels.
Admit them. Admit them.

This is confidence in the spirit of the night. It is evidence of a man who has wrestled with his soul. Similarly, the poet H. D., writing about a nightingale, begins in myrrh-wood and enchantment but pivots and turns the poem around on a heartbeat—actually the *heartbreak* of the sunlit world. The breaking of the heart, for her, is at least an opening. Any crack lets light through. For then she can say, "only night heals again, / only night heals again." Night heals in the way the soul is tempered, one degree, one battle at a time; the way consciousness is built, through steady struggles with forces older and greater than ourselves. How great is our faith in the regenerating powers of endarkenment? Can we believe that "in a dark time, the eye begins to see," as Theodore Roethke reassured a generation?

The midnight riders here have found ways to hold fast during those fractious hours just before dawn. The Old Man of the Mountain, Lao Tzu, recommended contemplating the stars; the Benedictine monk Brother David Steindl-Rast encourages practicing gratefulness. The peripatetic poet Jack Gilbert writes in "The White Heart of God" of having "hopes for even the faintest evidence, / the presence of the Lord's least abundance." Moreover, he hopes of finding "love's alembic," a lovely image for the distilling of night's wisdom.

And still, the questions hover: Do we have an eye for the mysteries? Do we answer the knocking at the door at night? Can we draw warm love out of the cold hours of the night? The German poet Else Lasker-Schüler believes in the lucent possibilities, the light-giving moments, the desire for uplifting. She writes, "We want to wake through the night / To pray in languages / Notched like harps. / We want to be reconciled with the night— / God overflows so much."

The soul of the night is there in the reconciliation, there where our beliefs "cleave us to the bone," as James Salter describes a bout with solitude in *A Sport and a Pastime*. It is there when we have the eyes to read the black ink on the dark paper of night, the time when "darkness is visible," as William Styron described his struggle with depression. For Styron there was great consolation in recalling how Dante's descent into the underworld ended. Only after Dante had forged his way through the dark wood and harrowed hell with his mentor, Vergil, could he write:

> *E quindi uscimmo a riveder le stelle.*
> And so we came forth, and once again beheld the stars.

The Holy Longing

> Tell a wise person, or else keep silent,
> because the massman will mock it right away.
> I praise what is truly alive,
> what longs to be burned to death.
>
> In the calm water of the love-nights,
> where you were begotten, where you have begotten,

a strange feeling comes over you
when you see the silent candle burning.

Now you are no longer caught
in the obsession with darkness,
and a desire for higher love-making
sweeps you upward.

Distance does not make you falter,
now, arriving in magic, flying,
and, finally, insane for the light,
you are the butterfly and you are gone.

And so long as you haven't experienced
this: to die and so to grow,
you are only a troubled guest
on the dark earth.

Johann Wolfgang von Goethe, 1749–1832
translated from German by Robert Bly

Out of the Dark Wood

For those who have dwelt in depression's dark wood, and
known its inexplicable agony, their return from the abyss
is not unlike the ascent of the poet, trudging upward and
upward out of hell's black depths and at last emerging into

what he saw as "the shining world." There, whoever has been restored to health has almost always been restored to the capacity for serenity and joy, and this may be indemnity enough for having endured the despair beyond despair.

> *E quindi uscimmo a riveder le stelle.*
> *And so we came forth, and once again beheld the stars.*

> William Styron

from Self-Reliance

> Trust thyself: every heart vibrates to that iron string. Accept the place the Divine Providence has found for you, the society of your contemporaries, the connection of events. Great men have always done so, and confided themselves child-like to the genius of their age, betraying their perception that the absolutely trustworthy was seated at their heart, working through their hands, predominating in all their being. And we are now men and must accept in the highest mind the same transcendent destiny; and not minors and invalids in a protected corner, not cowards fleeing before a revolution, but guides, redeemers, and benefactors, obeying the Almighty effort and advancing on Chaos and the Dark.

> *Ralph Waldo Emerson,* 1803–1882

Hold On in the Darkness

Hold on in the darkness though no gleam of light breaks
    through.
Keep on dreaming dreams although they never quite come
    true.
Keep on moving forward though you don't know what's
    ahead.
Keep on keeping on though it's a lonely road ahead.

Keep on looking up towards the goal you have in view.
Keep on at the task God has given you to do.
Keep on in the hope that there are better times in store.
Keep on praying for the thing that you are waiting for.

Blessings come to those who in the turmoil of events
Seek to see the goodness of the Will of Providence.
Hold to this and never doubt. Keep head and spirits high.
You'll discover that the storm was only passing by.

Seek Love in the pity of another's woe,
In the gentle relief of another's care.
In the darkness of night and the winter's snow.
In the naked and outcast—seek love there.

    Anonymous

from Meditations

All the blessings which you pray to obtain hereafter could be yours today, if you did not deny them to yourself. You have only to have done with the past altogether, commit the future to providence, and simply seek to direct the present hour aright into the paths of holiness and justice: holiness, by a loving acceptance of your apportioned lot, since Nature produced it for you and you for it: justice, in your speech by a frank and straightforward truthfulness, and in your acts by a respect for law and for every man's rights. Allow yourself, too, no hindrance from the malice, misconceptions or slanders of others, nor yet from any sensations this fleshy frame may feel; its afflicted part will look to itself. The hour for your departure draws near; if you will but forget all else and pay sole regard to the helmsman of your soul and the divine spark within you—if you will but exchange your fear of having to end your life some day for a fear of failing even to begin it on nature's true principles—you can yet become a man, worthy of the universe that gave you birth, instead of a stranger in your own homeland, bewildered by each day's happenings as though by wonders unlooked for, and ever hanging upon this one or the next.

Marcus Aurelius, 121–180
translated from Latin by Maxwell Staniforth

Once Calmed

Do you imagine the universe is agitated?
Go into the desert at night and look out at the stars.
This practice should answer the question.

The superior person settles her mind as the universe
    settles the stars in the sky.
By connecting her mind with the subtle origin, she
    calms it.
Once calmed, it naturally expands, and ultimately her
    mind becomes as vast and immeasurable as the
    night sky.

> *Lao Tzu,* c. 600 B.C.E.
> version from Chinese by Brian Walker

◑

Before Turning Off the Lights

Is there a method for cultivating mindfulness? There are
many methods. The one I have chosen is gratefulness, which
can be practiced, cultivated, learned. And as we grow in
gratefulness, we grow in mindfulness. Before I open my eyes
in the morning, I remind myself that I have eyes to see while
millions of my brothers and sisters are blind—most because

of conditions that could be improved if our human family would come to its senses and spend its resources reasonably, equitably. If I open my eyes with this thought, chances are that I will be more grateful for the gift of sight and more alert to the needs of those who lack that gift. Before I turn off the light in the evening, I jot down one thing for which I have never before been grateful. I have done this for years, and the supply still seems inexhaustible.

Gratefulness brings joy to my life. How could I find joy in what I take for granted? So I stop "taking for granted," and there is no end to the surprises I find. A grateful attitude is a creative one, because, in the final analysis, opportunity is the gift within the gift of every moment—the opportunity to see and hear and smell and touch and taste with pleasure.

There is no closer bond than the one that gratefulness celebrates, the bond between giver and thanksgiver. Everything is a gift. Grateful living is a celebration of the universal give-and-take of life, a limitless yes to belonging.

Can our world survive without gratefulness? Whatever the answer, one thing is certain: to say an unconditional yes to the mutual belonging of all beings will make this a more joyful world. This is the reason why yes is my favorite synonym for God.

Brother David Steindl-Rast

Where Is the Nightingale

Where is the nightingale,
in what myrrh-wood and dim?
Oh, let the night come black
for we would conjure back
all that enchanted him,
    all that enchanted him.

Where is the bird of fire,
in what packed hedge of rose?
in what roofed ledge of flower?
no other creature knows
what magic lurks within,
    what magic lurks within.

Bird, bird, bird, bird we cry,
hear, pity us in pain,
hearts break in the sunlight,
hearts break in the daylight rain,
only night heals again,
    only night heals again.

H. D. (Hilda Doolittle), 1886–1961

Lead, Kindly Light

Lead, kindly Light, amid the encircling gloom,
Lead thou me on;
The night is dark, and I am far from home,
Lead thou me on.
Keep thou my feet; I do not ask to see
The distant scene; one step enough for me.

I was not ever thus, nor prayed that thou
Shouldst lead me on;
I loved to choose and see my path; but now
Lead thou me on.
I loved the garish day, and, spite of fears,
Pride ruled my will: remember not past years.

So long thy power hath blest me, sure it still
Will lead me on
O'er moor and fen, o'er crag and torrent, till
The night is gone,
And with the morn those Angel faces smile,
Which I have loved long since, and lost awhile.

John Henry Newman, 1801–1890

The Gentle Rapping

Often in the stillness of the night, when all nature seems
asleep about me, there comes a gentle rapping at the door
of my heart. I open it; and a voice inquires, "Pokagon, what
of your people? What will their future be?" My answer is:
"Mortal man has not the power to draw aside the veil of
unborn time to tell the future of his race. That gift belongs
of the Divine alone. But it is given to him to closely judge
the future by the present, and the past."

Simon Pokagon, Potawatomie, 1830–1899

Peace

Night arches England, and the winds are still;
Jasmine and honeysuckle steep the air;
Softly the stars that are all Europe's fill
Her heaven-wide dark with radiancy fair;
That shadowed moon now waxing in the west,
Stirs not a rumor in her tranquil seas;
Mysterious sleep has lulled her heart to rest,
Deep even as theirs beneath her churchyard trees.

Secure, serene; dumb now the nighthawk's threat;
The gun's low thunder drumming o'er the tide;

The anguish pulsing in her stricken side . . .
All is at peace. Ah, never, heart, forget
For this her youngest, best, and bravest died,
These bright dews once were mixed with blood and sweat.

Walter de la Mare, 1873–1956

Human Wisdom

Human wisdom says, Don't put off until tomorrow
what can be done the same day.
But I tell you that he who knows how to put off until
    tomorrow
is the most agreeable to God.
He who sleeps like a child
is also he who sleeps like my darling Hope.
And I tell you, Put off until tomorrow
those worries and those troubles which are gnawing at
    you today,
and might very well devour you today.
Put off until tomorrow those tears that choke you
when you see today's unhappiness,
those sobs that rise up and strangle you.
Put off until tomorrow those tears which fill your eyes and
    your head

flooding you, rolling down your cheeks.
Because between now and tomorrow, maybe I, God,will
     have passed by your way . . .
Blessed is he who puts off, that is to say,
Blessed is he who hopes. And who sleeps.

Charles Péguy, 1873–1914

◗

The Starlight Night

Look at the stars! look, look up at the skies!
O look at all the fire-folk sitting in the air!
The bright boroughs, the circle-citadels there!
Down in dim woods the diamond delves! the elves'-eyes!
The gray lawns cold where gold, where quickgold lies!
Wind-beat whitebeam! airy abeles set on a flare!
Flake-doves sent floating forth at farmyard scare!
Ah, well! it is all a purchase, all is a prize.

Buy then! bid then!—What?—Prayer, patience, alms, vows.
Look, look a May-mess, like on orchard boughs!
Look! March-bloom, like on mealed-with-yellow sallows!
These are indeed the barn; withindoors house
The shocks. This piece-bright paling shuts the spouse
Christ home, Christ and his mother and all his hallows.

Gerard Manley Hopkins, 1844–1889

Solitude

Solitude. One knows instinctively it has benefits that must be more deeply satisfying than those of other conditions, but still it is difficult. And besides, how is one to distinguish between conditions which are valuable, which despite their hatefulness give us strength or impel us to great things and others we would be far better free of? Which are precious and which are not? Why is it so hard to be happy alone? Why is it impossible? . . .

I have not gone deep enough, that's the thing. In solitude one must penetrate, one must endure. The icy beginning is where it is worst. One must pass all that. One must go forward all the way, through bitterness, through righteous feelings, advancing upon it like a holy city, sensing the true joy. I try to summon it to me, to make it appear. I am certain it is there, but it does not come easily. Of course not. One must waver. One must struggle. Beliefs are meant to cleave us to the bone.

James Salter

●

In a Dark Time

In a dark time, the eye begins to see,
I meet my shadow in the deepening shade;

I hear my echo in the echoing wood—
A lord of nature weeping to a tree.
I live between the heron and the wren,
Beasts of the hill and serpents of the den.

What's madness but nobility of soul
At odds with circumstance? The day's on fire!
I know the purity of pure despair,
My shadow pinned against a sweating wall.
That place among the rocks—is it a cave,
Or winding path? The edge is what I have.

A steady storm of correspondences!
A night flowing with birds, a ragged moon,
And in broad day the midnight come again!
A man goes far to find out what he is—
Death of the self in a long, tearless night,
All natural shapes blazing unnatural light.

Dark, dark my light, and darker my desire.
My soul, like some heat-maddened summer fly,
Keeps buzzing at the sill. Which I is *I*?
A fallen man, I climb out of my fear.
The mind enters itself, and God the mind,
And one is One, free in the tearing wind.

Theodore Roethke, 1908–1963

from Song of a Man Who Has Come Through

Not I, not I, but the wind that blows through me!
A fine wind is blowing the new direction of Time.
If only I let it bear me, carry me, if only it carry me!
If only I am sensitive, subtle, oh, delicate, a winged gift!
If only, most lovely of all, I yield myself and am borrowed
By the fine, fine wind that takes its course through the chaos
    of the world

Like a fine, an exquisite chisel, a wedge-blade inserted;
If only I am keen and hard like the sheer tip of a wedge
Driven by invisible blows,
The rock will split, we shall come at the wonder, we shall
find the Hesperides.
....

What is the knocking?
What is the knocking at the door in the night?
It is somebody wants to do us harm.

No, no, it is the three strange angels.
Admit them, admit them.

    D. H. Lawrence, 1885–1930

Reconciliation

A great star has fallen into my lap . . .
We want to wake through the night,

To pray in languages
Notched like harps.

We want to be reconciled with the night—
God overflows so much.

Our hearts are children,
They may rest tiredsweet.

And our lips want to kiss,
Why do you hesitate?

Do not join my heart to yours—
Always your blood reddens my cheeks.

We want to be reconciled with the night,
When we embrace, we do not die.

A great star has fallen into my lap.

Else Lasker-Schüler, 1869–1945
translated from German by Robert Alter

The Vast Night

Often I gazed at you in wonder: stood at the window begun
the day before, stood and gazed at you in wonder. As yet
the new city seemed forbidden to me, and the strange
unpersuadable landscape darkened as though
I didn't exist. Even the nearest Things
didn't care whether I understood them. The street
thrust itself up to the lamppost: I saw it was foreign.
Over there—a room, feelable, clear in the lamplight—,
I already took part; they noticed, and closed the shutters.
Stood. Then a child began crying. I knew what the mothers
all around, in the houses, were capable of—, and knew
the inconsolable origins of all tears.
Or a woman's voice sang and reached a little beyond
expectation, or downstairs an old man let out
a cough that was full of reproach, as though his body were
    right
and the gentler world mistaken. And then the hour
struck—, but I counted too late, it tumbled on past me.—
Like a new boy at school, who is finally allowed to join in,
but he can't catch the ball, is helpless at all the games
the others pursue with such ease, and he stands there staring
into the distance,—where—?: I stood there and suddenly
grasped that it was you: *you* were playing with me,
    grown-up

Night, and I gazed at you in wonder. Where the towers
were raging, where with averted fate
a city surrounded me, and indecipherable mountains
camped against me, and strangeness, in narrowing circles,
prowled around my randomly flickering emotions—:
it was then that in all your magnificence
you were not ashamed to know me. Your breath moved
    tenderly
over my face. And, spread across solemn distances,
your smile entered my heart.

Rainer Maria Rilke, 1875–1926
translated from German by Stephen Mitchell

◐

Dawn

I have spent a restless and sleepless night.
Day is dawning and I slip out of bed, bored.
Today I alone walk along this long street
of sealed doors and sleeping houses.

A dawn like smoke.
It seems the sun, ill-humored,
has lit a fire with green wood
to cook its breakfast.

The wind is moist like it just came from
a bath. In the pale sky,

the colorless stars
little by little are vanishing.

A milkman in a red beret goes by,
From atop an old wall,
I am tempted by a bent, plus branch
heavy with ripe medlars.

I walk, walk, walk, walk.
When I return and bend over him
With a kiss, to wake him,
He will think, with hungry joy,
That I too have just come from the bath.

> *Juana de Ibarbourou,* 1895–1979
> from *Raíz salvaje,* 1922
> translated from Spanish by Perry Higman

The Gift

This darkness is a rope, not a prison:
hand over hand I haul myself in
to touch your face, to blossom.

My fingers crawl toward heaven
leaving behind whorling shadows;
this darkness is a rope, not a prison.

I follow light through forgotten
canyons and grottos;
I touch your face and know

that even the sun has a mission:
as it climbs, it grows.
This darkness is a rope, not a prison

not a cell from which I hasten.
Freely, hand over hand I follow
to touch your face, to open and open

like a night-blooming jasmine,
or a well widening with echoes:
this darkness is a rope, not a prison,
I touch your face, I blossom.

Maurya Simon

The Night-Blooming Cereus

And so for nights
we waited, hoping to see
the heavy bud
break into flower.

On its neck-like tube
hooking down from the edge
of the leaf-branch
    nearly to the floor.

    the bud packed
tight with its miracle swayed
stiffly on breaths
    of air, moved

    as though impelled
by stirrings within itself.
It repelled as much
    as it fascinated me

    sometimes—snake,
eyeless bird head,
beak that would gape
    with grotesque life-squawk.

    But you, my dear,
conceded less to the bizarre
than to the imminence
    of bloom. Yet we agreed

    we ought
to celebrate the blossom,
paint ourselves, dance
    in honor of

archaic mysteries
when it appeared. Meanwhile
we waited, aware
        of rigorous design.

Backster's
polygraph, I thought,
would have shown
        (as clearly as it had

philodendron's
fear) tribal sentience
in the cactus, focused
        energy of will.

That belling of
tropic perfume—that
signaling
        not meant for us;

the darkness
cloyed with summoning
fragrance. We dropped
        trivial tasks

and marvelling
beheld at last the achieved
flower. Its moonlight
        petals were

still unfold-
ing, the spike fringe of the outer
perianth recessing
as we watched.

Lunar presence,
foredoomed, already dying,
it charged the room
with plangency

older than human
cries, ancient as prayers
invoking Osiris, Krishna,
Tezcátlipóca.

We spoke
in whispers when
we spoke
at all . . .

Robert Hayden

June Intercedes in the Garden of Roses

There is no hurry—no hurry today.
No one you love is going to die.

The huddled gold roses. The showy pink ones, bright-
pink, under a mackerel sky.

Was it irrevocable loss that kept you awake
last night? Fear of irrevocable loss?

The huddled gold roses, the showy pink ones bright-
white. Like

her mother's letters, in plain writing,
in their envelopes, that she saved:

those were the things that made
her cry.

That grief has now been placed
at a remove.

But the rose that's queen of the May, the June, July,
was already planted by human hands. It can contain

this. No church, no figure of speech, can make you love
actual loss.

The peach-down roses, splayed single-petals wavery,
    fragrant,
near white.

Was it the fear of loss
that kept you awake last night?

There's no hurry, no hurry, today.
No one you love is going to die.

Elizabeth Macklin

Night Stock

Once I was called from sleep by scented stock,
purple and white clusters flooding the dark:
I stood in moonlight converting the scent
into a childhood association
of passing quickly through gardens at night,
the sea behind me, and aware
between the terror I shouldn't be there,
and lights sunk into laurels, of a catch,
a fragrance to my fear, and years later
discovering that companion as stock.

Perhaps I went outside from delayed shock,
motivated by dream to conciliate
an old scar with the present. Hurried moths
were spotting on the air. I looked back in,
imagining a light around my bed
and that the sleeper dreamt the incident,
and that I'd wake to find myself assured
I hadn't moved.

I bent to inhale flowers,
the stock too potent for jasmine,
kneaded the damp grass with my hands and feet,
and went back in, confident I could claim
the brief living experience for mine.

Jeremy Reed

◑

The Night View of the World

"Upon the night view of the world, a day view must follow."
This is an ancient insight grounded in the experience of the
race in its long journey through all the years of man's be-
coming. Here is no cold idea born out of the vigil of some
solitary thinker in lonely retreat from the traffic of the com-
mon ways. It is not the wisdom of the book put down in
ordered words by the learned and the schooled. It is insight
woven into the pattern of all living things, reaching its grand
apotheosis in the reflection of man gazing deep into the
heart of his own experience.

That the day view follows the night view is written large
in nature. Indeed it is one with nature itself. The clouds
gather heavy with unshed tears; at last they burst, sending
over the total landscape waters gathered from the silent
offering of sea and river. The next day dawns and the whole
heavens are aflame with the glorious brilliance of the sun.

This is the way the rhythm moves. The fall of the year comes, then winter with its trees stripped of leaf and bud; cold winds ruthless in bitterness and sting. One day there is sleet and ice; in the silence of the nighttime the snow falls soundlessly—all this until at last the cold seems endless and all there is seems to be shadowy and foreboding. The earth is weary and heavy. Then something stirs—a strange new vitality pulses through everything. One can feel the pressure of some vast energy pushing, always pushing through dead branches, slumbering roots—life surges everywhere within and without. Spring has come. The day usurps the night view.

Is there any wonder that deeper than idea and concept is the insistent conviction that the night can never stay, that winter is ever moving toward the spring? Thus, when a man sees the lights go out one by one, when he sees the end of his days marked by death—his death—he *senses,* rather than knows, that even the night into which he is entering will be followed by day. It remains for religion to give this ancient wisdom phrase and symbol. For millions of men and women in many climes this phrase and this symbol are forever one with Jesus, the Prophet from Galilee. When the preacher says as a part of the last rites, "I am the Resurrection and the Life, . . ." he is reminding us all of the ancient wisdom: "Upon the night view of the world, a day view must follow."

Howard Thurman, 1900–1981

The Grandeur of a New Sunrise

Is life an open road or a blind alley? This question, barely formulated a few centuries ago, is today explicitly on the lips of mankind as a whole. As a result of the brief, violent moment of crisis in which it became conscious at once of its creative power and of its critical faculties, humanity has quite legitimately become hard to move: no stimulus at the level of mere instinct or blind economic necessity will suffice for long to goad it into moving onwards. Only a reason, and a valid and important reason, for loving life passionately will cause it to advance further. But where, at the experiential level, are we to find, if not a complete justification, at least the beginnings of a justification of life? Only, it would seem, in the consideration of the intrinsic value of the phenomenon of man. Continue to regard man as an accidental outgrowth or sport of nature and you will drive him into a state of disgust or revolt which, if it became general, would mean the definitive stoppage of life on earth. Recognize, on the other hand, that within the domain of our experience man is at the head of one of the two greatest waves into which, for us, tangible reality is divided, and that therefore he holds in his hands the fortunes of the universe: and immediately you cause him to turn his face towards the grandeur of a new sunrise.

Man has every right to be anxious about his fate so long as he feels himself to be lost and lonely in the midst of the

mass of created things. But let him once discover that his
fate is bound up with the fate of nature itself, and immedi-
ately, joyously, he will begin again his forward march. For
it would denote in him not a critical sense but a malady of
the spirit if he were doubtful of the value and the hopes
of an entire world.

Pierre Teilhard de Chardin, 1881–1955
translated from French by Simon Bartholomew

The White Heart of God

The snow falling around the man in the naked woods
is like the ash of heaven, ash from the cool fire
of God's mother-of-pearl, moon-stately heart.
Sympathetic but not merciful. His strictness
parses us. The discomfort of living this way
without birds, among maples without leaves, makes
death and the world visible. Not the harshness,
but the way this world can be known by pushing
against it. And feeling something pushing back.
The whiteness of the winter married to this river
makes the water look black. The water actually
is the color of giant mirrors set along the marble
corridors of the spirit, the mirrors empty
of everything. The man is doing the year's accounts.

Finding the balance, trying to estimate how much
he has been translated. For it does translate him,
well or poorly. As the woods are translated
by the seasons. He is searching for a base line
of the Lord. He searches like the blind man
going forward with a hand stretched out in front.
As the truck driver ice-fishing on the big pond
tries to learn from his line what is down there.
The man attends to any signal that might announce
Jesus. He hopes for even the faintest evidence,
the presence of the Lord's least abundance. He measures
with tenderness, afraid to find a heart more classical
than ripe. Hoping for honey, for love's alembic.

Jack Gilbert

◗

The Still Time

I know there is still time—
time for the hands
to open, for the bones of them
to be filled
by those failed harvests of want,
the bread imagined of the days of not having.

Now that the fear
has been rummaged down to its husk,
and the wind blowing
the flesh away translates itself
into flesh and the flesh
gives itself in its reveries to the wind.

I remember those summer nights
when I was young and empty,
when I lay through the darkness
wanting, wanting,
knowing
I would have nothing of anything I wanted—
that total craving
that hollows the heart out irreversibly.

So it surprises me now to hear
the steps of my life following me—
so much of it gone
it returns, everything that drove me crazy
comes back, blessing the misery
of each step it took me into the world;
as though a prayer had ended
and the bit of changed air
between the palms goes free
to become the glitter
on some common thing that inexplicably shines.

And the old voice,
which once made its broken-off, choked, parrot-
    incoherences,
speaks again,
this time on the palatum cordis,
this time saying there is time, still time,
for one who can groan
to sing,
for one who can sing to be healed.

              Galway Kinnell

◗

"Before Dawn . . ."

Before dawn there you lie
sleepwalking circles in
your particularly nil
corner of eternity where

each routine circuit of
the mind plants another
iron pillar of thought around
which the next circuit's routed;

no change, no relief appears;
then, with a kick from ancient

energy of sun coming
up somewhere, sleep—sent to release

the hapless circuit traveler
from his pains—bears the
next instant into dream
fields of freedom; and life

happens to you all over again
in a way that, outside the moon cavern,
cannot be spoken of,
or thought, or named.

Tom Clark

Phantasmagoria

One winter night, at half-past nine,
     Cold, tired, and cross, and muddy,
I had come home, too late to dine,
And supper, with cigars and wine,
     Was waiting in the study.

There was a strangeness in the room,
     And Something white and wavy
Was standing near me in the gloom—

I took it for the carpet-broom
     Left by that careless slavey.

But presently the Thing began
     To shiver and to sneeze:
On which I said "Come, come, my man!
That's a most inconsiderate plan,
     Less noise there, if you please!"

"I've caught a cold," the Thing replies,
     "Out there upon the landing."
I turned to look in some surprise,
And there, before my very eyes,
     A Little Ghost was standing!

When encountering a ghost for the first time it is necessary
to remain as calm as may be and to retain the normal courte-
sies of civilized society, viz. on meeting a ghost in the street
after dark a gentleman should *always* raise his hat. However
should you be lying in bed affeared lest you might meet a
ghost, having never met one before, the simplest method
of allaying those fears is to conjure up a shadowy ghost of
your own.

I dreamt I dwelt in marble halls,
And each damp thing that creeps and crawls
Went wobble-wobble on the walls.

By positioning your hands so as to form certain configura-
tions and by placing your hands between a source of light—

be it a moonbeam or a lamp—and a blank wall, you can ensure that what goes wobble-wobble on your bedroom wall is not a fiend but a friend.

Charles Lutwidge Dodgson (Lewis Carroll), 1832–1898

Sleepwalking

There are some bizarre stories about sleepwalking. I think we have all heard of the lady, guest in a great house, who woke in the small hours to hear the breathing and moving of a male presence. On the coverlet she could feel objects being placed in order and with deliberation. She did not dare stir. Wisely she fainted. She came to at dawn to find that the butler had walked in his sleep and laid the table for fourteen on her bed. Lawrence Wright, the bed expert, tells of the baronet in Hampshire who went to bed every night in a shirt and every morning woke stark naked. There was no trace of the garment anywhere. After hundreds of shirts had disappeared in this way, he asked a friend to watch over his sleep. The friend did so and, as the clock struck one, observed the baronet get out of bed, light a candle, and walk out of the room. The friend followed him a fair distance to the stable-yard, where the baronet took off his shirt and, using a pitchfork, buried it in a dungheap. He then returned, still fast asleep, to his naked bed.

One morning I got up to find the following verses
scrawled in lipstick on my dining-room wall:
Let his carbon gnoses be up right
And wak all folowers to his light
The writing was my own and the lipstick my wife's.
Some people talk of the inspiration of sleep and assert that
there is great wisdom to be tapped in the unconscious mind.
If this couplet is a specimen of this wisdom let me stay
conscious. I knew a man who woke up in the night to find
he had discovered in sleep the key to the universe. He
scrawled on a pad kept on his bedside table the mystical
unlocking words. Waking he read them: "All a matter of
demisemiquavers. Make much of this."

Anthony Burgess, 1917–1993

Night Wood (Duo)

Miss Djuna Barnes:
"So I say—what of the night—
the terrible night?"

Poor Anna:
"What of the night? The night's all right!
Pain and Pox

Come at all o'clocks,
But chiefly delight, through the happy night.
Darling, take heart,
Make hay, make a start,
Learn Peace, learn Power
From the zero hour."

Anna Wickham, 1884–1947

The Peace of Wild Things

When despair for the world grows in me
and I wake in the night at the least sound
in fear of what my life and my children's lives may be,
I go and lie down where the wood drake
rests in his beauty on the water, and the great heron feeds.
I come into the peace of wild things
who do not tax their lives with forethought
of grief. I come into the presence of still water.
And I feel above me the day-blind stars
waiting with their light. For a time
I rest in the grace of the world, and am free.

Wendell Berry

Demeter

In your dream you met Demeter
Splendid and severe, who said: Endure.
Study the art of seeds,
The nativity of caves.
Dance your gay body to the poise of waves;
Die out of the world to bring forth the obscure
Into blisses, into needs.
In all resources
Belong to love. Bless,
Join, fashion the deep forces,
Asserting your nature, priceless and feminine.
Peace, daughter. Find your true kin.
        —then you felt her kiss.

Genevieve Taggard, 1894–1948

The Hush of Dawn

In his seventeenth-century play, *La Vida es Sueño* (Life's a Dream), Pedro Calderón de la Barca anticipated much of today's magic realism and surrealist literature. Writing as hypnotically as Borges or Marquez would two centuries later, Calderón revealed that when he slept . . . he saw . . . that he dreamt . . . when he was awake. . . .

> We live in a world so strange,
> That to live is only to dream.
> He who lives, dreams his life
> Until he wakes. This much
> Experience has taught me.

So what *does* transpire during the night? *Who* were you? *Where* were you? *What* have you brought back from your elliptical night journey? "Is the rising light daybreak," asks the Persian poet Bibi Hayati, "or the reflection of your face?" Is Coach in *Cheers* just crazy or madly inspired when he confides to bartender Sam, "I think I had insomnia last night, but I don't remember because I fell asleep"?

Why can't we stay awake to remember what we forgot?

Though often ravished by the terrific forces of despair, Nietzsche persevered through his faith in creation: "And how could I endure to be a man, if man were not also a poet and reader of riddles . . . a way to new dawns."

For those in this final part, "the morning hour has gold in its mouth," as imagined in the old German proverb. Night has been endured, outlasted. The morning star flickers on the horizon. Slowly, bewilderedly, we emerge from the shadowlands. In "the hour-before-dawn dark" the world is "megalith-still," says poet Ted Hughes in "The Horses." Federico García Lorca's memory in "Night" is of "little windows of gold / trembling. . . ." Night contains day in a mysterious manner. The glimmer of dawn itself is an omen for the Finnish poet Edith Södergran. For her, when the sky pales, "you have the faintest presentiment of the day beginning / in the darkness."

On the morning of his sacred vision, the Oglala Sioux shaman and missionary Black Elk heard the sun singing as it arose and felt it calling for a song from him. Strengthened by his lifted voice, he foresaw that by walking in a sacred manner he could say, "My day, I have made it holy."

In "The Daled" Louis Simpson's card players are making the night holy; to "play right through till dawn" is a wonderful metaphor for understanding the elusive truth of the lessons of light and dark. The search through the "ashes of night" is a search for metaphors, and in the ashes of another's fire Noah benShea's Jacob finds consolation that "somebody else has been in the night . . . and somebody else has carried on." From the Russian poet Anna Akhmatova we learn to take our darkness lessons, to "take from the left and from the right . . . and everything—from the silence of the night."

The night is like the art of falconry. The strong life force in our grip must be trained, then released, with faith in its returning, out of an admixture of love, cunning, hunger, and a strengthening by the light. The night journey is a flight of faith. A belief that what goes around comes around. "We are such stuff / As dreams are made of," wrote the Bard in *The Tempest,* "and our little life / Is rounded with a sleep."

To what prayers and poetry, what cries from the heart and praise from the soul, will we listen, if not these, if not now, as dawn is breaking, once more?

from Songs of Owl Woman

The Dawn Approaches

I am afraid it will be daylight before I reach the place to see.
I feel that the rays of the sun are striking me.

The Morning Star

The morning star is up.
I cross the mountains into the light of the sea.

> *Owl Woman (Juana Manwell),* fl. 1880?
> translated from Papago by Frances Densmore

Wake!

Wake! For the Sun who scatter'd into flight
The Stars before him from the Field of Night,
Drives Night along with them from Heaven and strikes
The Sultán's Turret with a Shaft of Light.

from The Rubáiyát of Omar Khayyám
translated by Edward Fitzgerald

Dawn Prayer

Father-Creator, Provider-from-old, Ancient-of-days—fresh-born from the womb of night are we. In the first dawning of the new day draw we nigh unto thee. Forlorn are the eyes till they've seen the Chief.

South African Bushman

Night

Candle, lamp,
lantern and firefly.

The constellation
of the dart.

Little windows of gold
trembling,
and cross upon cross
rocking in the dawn.

Candle, lamp,
lantern and firefly.

Federico García Lorca, 1898–1936
translated from Spanish by Jaime de Angulo

Lying Single in Bed

Rode easily to Welling, where we supped well, and had two
beds in the room and so lay single, and still remember it of
all nights that ever I slept in my life I never did pass a night
with more epicurism of sleep; there being now and then a
noise of people stirring that waked me, and then it was a
very rainy night, and then I was a little weary, that what
between waking and sleeping again, one after another, I
never had so much content in all my life, and so my wife
says it was with her.

Samuel Pepys, 1633–1703

The Sweetest Night

Last night was the sweetest night I ever had in my life. I never before, for so long a time together, enjoyed so much of the light and rest and sweetness of heaven in my soul. . . . Part of the night I lay awake, sometimes asleep, and sometimes between sleeping and waking. But all night I continued in a constant, clear, and lively sense of the heavenly sweetness of Christ's excellent love, of his nearness to me, and of my dearness to him; with an inexpressibly sweet calmness of soul in an entire rest in him. I seemed to myself to perceive a glow of divine love come down from the heart of Christ in heaven into my heart in a constant stream, like a stream or pencil of sweet light. . . . At the same time my heart and soul all flowed out in love to Christ, so that there seemed to be a constant flowing and reflowing of heavenly love, and I appeared to myself to float or swim, in these bright, sweet beams, like the motes swimming in the beams of the sun, or the streams of his light which come in at the window. I think that what I felt each minute was worth more than all the outward comfort and pleasure which I had enjoyed in my whole life put together. It was pleasure, without the least sting, or any interruption. It was a sweetness, which my soul was lost in; it seemed to be all that my feeble frame could sustain. There was but little difference, whether I was asleep or awake, but if there was any difference, the sweetness was greatest while I was asleep.

Mrs. Jonathan Edwards, 18th century

Early Dawn

Some stars shining weakly.
I see them out of my window. The sky is pale,
you have the faintest presentiment of the day beginning
           in the darkness.
A silence rests outspread on the lake,
there's a whispering lying in wait between the trees,
my old garden listens half distracted
to the night's breath, sighing over the road.

Edith Södergran, 1892–1923
translated from Finnish by Samuel Charters

Hearing the Sun Singing

And as I walked alone, I heard the sun singing as it arose,
and it sang like this:

"With visible face I am appearing.
In a sacred manner I appear.
For the greening earth a pleasantness I make.
The center of the nation's hoop I have made pleasant.
With visible face, behold me!
The four-leggeds and two-leggeds, I have made them to
        walk;

The wings of the air, I have made them to fly.
With visible face I appear.
My day, I have made it holy."

Black Elk, Oglala Sioux, 1863–1950

The Advancing Dawn

In the life of the Indian there was only one inevitable duty,—
the duty of prayer—the daily recognition of the Unseen and
Eternal. His daily devotions were more necessary to him
than daily food. He wakes at daybreak, puts on his moc-
casins and steps down to the water's edge. Here he throws
handfuls of clear, cold water into his face, or plunges in
bodily. After the bath, he stands erect before the advancing
dawn, facing the sun as it dances upon the horizon, and
offers his unspoken orison. His mate may precede or follow
him in his devotions, but never accompanies him. Each soul
must meet the morning sun, the new sweet earth and the
Great Silence alone!

Whenever, in the course of the daily hunt the red hunter
comes upon a scene that is strikingly beautiful or sublime—
a black thundercloud with the rainbow's glowing arch above
the mountain, a white waterfall in the heart of a green gorge;
a vast prairie tinged with the blood-red of sunset—he pauses
for an instant in the attitude of worship. He sees no need

for setting apart one day in seven as a holy day, since to him all days are God's.

Ohiyesa *(Charles Alexander Eastman)*, Dakota Sioux,
1858–1939

To Tan Ch'iu

My friend is lodging high in the Eastern Range,
Dearly loving the beauty of valleys and hills.
At green Spring he lies in the empty woods,
And is still asleep when the sun shines on high.
A pine-tree wind dusts his sleeves and coat;
A pebbly stream cleans his heart and ears.
I envy you, who far from strife and talk
Are high propped on a pillow of blue cloud.

Li Po, 701–762
translated from Chinese by Arthur Waley

I Sought My Lover at Twilight

I sought my lover at twilight
Snow fell at daybreak.
Residing at the Potala
I am Rigdzin Tsangyang Gyatso

But in the back alleys of Shol-town
I am rake and stud.
Secret or not
No matter.
Footprints have been left in the snow.

Tsangyang Gyatso, Tibet's Sixth Dalai Lama, 1683–1706
translated from Tibetan by Rick Fields

◗

A Riddling Tale

Three women were transformed into flowers which grew in the field, but one of them was allowed to be in her own home at night. Then once when day was drawing near, and she was forced to go back to her companions in the field and become a flower again, she said to her husband: "If you will come this afternoon and gather me, I shall be set free and henceforth stay with you." And he did so. Now the question is, how did her husband know her, for the flowers were exactly alike, and without any difference? Answer: as she was at her home during the night and not in the field, no dew fell on her as it did on the others, and by this her husband knew her.

The Grimm Brothers, 1785–1859
translated from German by Margaret Hunt
and revised by James Stern

Is This Darkness the Night of Power

Is this darkness the night of Power, or the black falling of
   your hair?
Is the rising light daybreak, or the reflection of your face?

In the book of Beauty, is this a first line?
Or merely a fragment I scribble, tracing your eyebrows?

Is this boxwood gathered in the orchard, or the rose garden's
   cypress?
The Tree of Paradise, heavy with dates, or the shape of your
   standing?

Is this scent from a Chinese deer, or the fragrance of infused
   water?
Is it the breathing of roses carried on wind, or your perfume?

Is this scorching a lightning bolt's remnants, or the burning
   mountain?
The heat of my sighs, or your inner body?

Is this Mongolian musk, or the purest of ambergris?
Is it the hyacinth unfolding, or your plaited curls?

Is this magic, or a chalice of red wine at dawn?
Your narcissus eye drunk with the way, or a sorcerer's work?

Is it the garden of Eden, or some earthly paradise?
The temple of those who have mastered the hear, or an
   alley?

Others all turn toward adobe and mud when they pray to the
    Sacred—
The temple of Hayati's soul turns toward the sun of your
    Face.

> *Bibi Hayati,* ?–1853
> translated from Persian by Jane Hirshfield

The Night at Zenshō-ji Temple

I spent the night at a temple called Zenshō-ji on the outskirts
of the town of Daishōji. I was still in the province of Kaga.
Sora had stayed at the temple the night before and had left a
poem:

> All through the night
>   I listened to the autumn wind
>   In the lonely hills.

We were only one night apart, but it seemed like a
thousand miles. I, too, listened to the autumn wind as I lay
awake. As dawn approached, I could hear the priests chant-
ing. Then a gong sounded and we all went in to the refectory.
Since I wanted to reach Echizen Province that same day,
I started to leave in a great hurry, but a young monk came
running down the steps after me with some paper and an

ink stone. Just then, some leaves from a willow tree in the garden fluttered to the ground.

> Your kindness to repay,
>   Would I might sweep the fallen
>   Willow leaves away!

My straw sandals were already tied on, so I did not even take the time to read over my hurried lines.

Matsuo Bashō, 1644–1694
translated from Japanese by Dorothy Britton

The Horses

I climbed through woods in the hour-before-dawn dark.
Evil air, a frost-making stillness,

Not a leaf, not a bird,—
A world cast in frost. I came out above the wood

Where my breath left tortuous statues in the iron light.
But the valleys were draining the darkness

Till the moorline—blackening dregs of the brightening grey—
Halved the sky ahead. And I saw the horses:

Huge in the dense grey—ten together—
Megalith-still. They breathed, making no move,

With draped manes and tilted hind-hooves,
Making no sound.

I passed: not one snorted or jerked its head.
Grey silent fragments

Of a grey silent world.

I listened in emptiness on the moor-ridge.
The curlew's tear turned its edge on the silence.

Slowly detail leafed from the darkness. Then the sun
Orange, red, red erupted.

Silently, and splitting to its core tore and flung cloud,
Shook the gulf open, showed blue,

And the big planets hanging—
I turned

Stumbling in the fever of a dream, down towards
The dark woods, from the kindling tops,

And came to the horses.
                          There, still they stood,
But now steaming and glistening under the flow of light,

Their draped stone manes, their tilted hind-hooves
Stirring under a thaw while all around them

The frost showed its fires. But still they made no sound.
Not one snorted or stamped,

Their hung heads patient as the horizons
High over valleys, in the red levelling rays—

In din of the crowded streets, going among the years, the
    faces,
May I still meet my memory in so lonely a place

Between the streams and the red clouds, hearing curlews,
Hearing the horizons endure.

Ted Hughes

The Daled

Across the room the night city editor
has turned his face toward me
with a curious, mild stare.
Waiting for copy . . .

Later in the evening there will be a crowd
at Jack's. Discussing sports . . .
Some old codger holding forth—
what His Honor said to the Commissioner.
And there will be the usual four.

According to an ancient fable
there are thirty-six "hidden saints."

It could be the tailor, the shoemaker,
it could be a Regular Army colonel—
as long as there are thirty-six
the world will not come to an end.

Also there are the Daled—four newspapermen
who are always playing poker.
As long as this situation continues
God will hold back the final catastrophe.
"What's that? It sounds like water."
"Wait a minute," says Shapiro.
"We're here to play cards. Whose deal is it?"

"I'll see your five," says Flanagan,
"and raise it."
                    So the game goes on
from week to week. I have known them to begin
late at night when everything is silent
and to play right through till dawn.

Louis Simpson

The Blind Watchmaker

Every night the blind watchmaker rewinds the day
He is repairing the broken mechanisms of silence
He is seizing the night. With cool blue light

in his flashpoint fingertips
he is feeling for the myriad ways
that time stops, fixing the rusted springs of
old timepieces, polishing infinitesimal
jewels, nudging darkness ahead into light
He is bending low over the grand complications,
gazing through the lens of his heart
at the gauzy movements that reveal
the infinite ways time is lost
He is murmuring, asking some-
thing of the dark source in the night,
the way flashlight beams do of
the strong force beyond
distant cloud nebulae
This is how he finds time,
by *snapping* open the hidden catch
When the watchmaker appears in my nightscapes
he guides my cramped hands along the
seized gears between dusk and dawn. He is teaching
me to feel in the creases of my calloused fingertips
the first moment of movement in the long-stilled
second hands of watches and clocks scattered
across his desk. Every night
the steady ratcheting forward
of things, the inexorable winding
down felt in the blueness of
my bones, in no time at all

like the timeless ways
you move me
in the held-breath
seconds just before dawn

Phil Cousineau

●

In the Ashes of Night

"Jacob, where do you find the strength to carry on in life?"

"Life is often heavy only because we attempt to carry it,"
said Jacob. "But, I do find a strength in the ashes."

"In the ashes?" asked Mr. Gold.

"Yes," said Jacob, with a confirmation that seemed to
have traveled a great distance.

"You see, Mr. Gold, each of us is alone. Each of us is in
the great darkness of our ignorance. And, each of us is on a
journey.

"In the process of our journey, we must bend to build
a fire for light, and warmth, and food.

"But when our fingers tear at the ground, hoping to find
the coals of another's fire, what we often find are the ashes.

"And, in these ashes, which will not give us light or
warmth, there may be sadness, but there is also testimony.

"Because these ashes tell us that somebody else has been in the night, somebody else has bent to build a fire, and somebody else has carried on.

"And that can be enough, sometimes."

Noah benShea

The Poet

You think this is working—
This is easy living:
To overhear some music,
And, joking, claim it as your own.

And, arranging someone's merry scherzo
Into lines of some sort,
To swear that some poor heart
Is moaning in a shining field of corn.

And afterwards to eavesdrop in the forest,
Among pines resembling nuns sworn to silence,
In a smoke-screen
Of hanging haze.

I take from the left and from the right,
And even, without feeling guilt,

A little bit from cunning life,
And everything—from the silence of the night.

Anna Akhmatova, 1888–1966
translated by Judith Hemschemeyer

from The Tempest

"Be cheerful, Sir.
Our revels are now ended. These our actors,
As I foretold you, were all spirits and
Are melted into air, into thin air;
And, like the baseless fabric of this vision,
The cloud-capp'd towers, the gorgeous palaces,
The solemn temples, the great globe itself,
Yea, all which it inherit, shall dissolve,
And, like this insubstantial pageant faded,
Leave not a rack behind. We are such stuff
As dreams are made of: and our little life
Is rounded with a sleep."

William Shakespeare, 1564–1616

Greeting to Day

To be spoken from bed, in the early morning, before anybody has risen.

I will rise from sleep
with the swiftness
of the raven's wingbeat.
I will rise to meet the day.
Wa-wa.

My face turns
from the darkness,
my eyes turn to meet
the dawn, whitening the sky.

Orpingalik
translated from Netsilki Eskimo by Tom Lowenstein

Deep peace of the running wave to you.
Deep peace of the flowing air to you.
Deep peace of the quiet earth to you.
Deep peace of the shining stars to you.
Deep peace of the Son of peace to you.

Celtic Benediction
Iona Community

Gratitudes

First thanks must go to my publishers, Tom and Mary Grady, for passing me the torch of their inspiration for an anthology of night writing that would appeal to restless souls still counting sheep at 3 A.M. or watching reruns of *Hawaii Five-0* at dawn. Let's hope this collection will help put people to sleep for all the right reasons.

My late-night gratitude is due to all those who helped me through the last year of all-nighters necessary for dreaming up this book. Those who've been generous with their gifts of stimulating conversation, caffeinated books, and literary cappuccinos include my nighthawk companions, Richard Beban and Keith Thompson, Cynthia Terra for teaching me how to juggle time, my sister, Nicole Cousineau-Black for her faith, love, and courage, my cousin Michael Cousineau for his care packages of Kona coffee, my brother, Paul Cousineau, with whom I've shared many a café table from Manila to Paris searching for the soul of the night, and cellist David Darling for the inspiration of his eight-stringed religion.

Soulful thanks Joyce Jenkins for her literary sleuthing, over-the-transom faxes, and unflagging encouragement. A drumbeat of appreciation to Gary Rhine, who guided me through my first Native American prayer meetings: *Aho!* And benedictions to my mother, Rosemary Cousineau, who first taught me the poetry of prayer, which I forgot about until I later saw the mystery of prayer in poetry, and to Sister Patricia Ann for all her prayers.

I'm also much obliged to my friends at HarperSanFrancisco, especially my editor, Caroline Pincus, whose exuberant support and gracious suggestions helped me "reconcile the darkness," Terri Goff for lighting the way of production editing, Mimi Kusch for her graceful threading of the manuscript through the maze, Michele Wetherbee for her deft art direction, Judy Beck for her attentiveness and enthusiasm, Deanna Quinones for going beyond the call of duty, Anne Hayes for her eleventh-hour help with the purgatory of permissions, and all the others on the Harper staff who collaborated on the production of this book.

Finally, my deep gratitude again to Jo Beaton, who was a prayer to my answers while I burned the candle at both ends, and an answer to my prayers while I burned the midnight oil.

Acknowledgments

The Rush of Darkness

Excerpt from "Songs of Owl Woman," by Owl Woman (Juana Manwell). Translated by Frances Densmore. From *Papago Music,* Bulletin 90 of the Bureau of American Ethnology. Published by the Smithsonian Institution. Copyright © 1929 by Frances Densmore.

"The Murmur of Night," from the *Popol Vuh.* Translated with commentary by Dennis Tedlock in *Popul Vuh.* Published by Simon & Schuster, Inc. Copyright © 1985 by Dennis Tedlock.

"The Birth of Night," from *Hesiod's Theogony.* Translated by Norman O. Brown. Copyright © 1953 by the Liberal Arts Press.

"Night Births," "A Tahitian Family Prayer," and "The Girl of the Early Race Who Made the Stars," from *Technicians of the Sacred,* by Jerome Rothenberg. Second edition, revised and expanded. Published by Univ. of California Press. Copyright © 1968, 1985 by Jerome Rothenberg.

"A Sudanese Evening Prayer," "A Shinto Evening Prayer," "Evening Hymn," attributed to St. Patrick, "At Evening," by Jacob Boehme, from *The Oxford Book of Prayer.* General editor, George Appleton. Oxford and New York: Oxford Univ. Press, 1988.

Excerpt from "The Navajo Song of the Earth," translated by Natalie Curtis Burlin. From *American Indian Poetry: An Anthology of Songs and Chants.* Edited by George W. Cronyn. New York: Ballantine Books, 1991. Copyright © renewed 1962 by George W. Cronyn.

"Evening Prayer," by Maulana Jalaluddin Rumi. From *I Am Wind, You Are Fire: The Life and Work of Rumi,* by Annemarie Schimmel. Copyright © 1992 by Annemarie Schimmel. Reprinted by arrangement with Shambhala Publications, Inc., P.O. Box 308, Boston, MA 02117.

"Be Thou My Vision," version by Mary Byrne from ancient Irish, and "Prayer," by George Herbert, from *The HarperCollins Book of Prayers.* Compiled by Robert Van de Weyer. San Francisco: HarperSanFrancisco, 1993.

"A Nocturnal Reverie," by Anne Finch, Countess of Winchilsea. Cited in *The Penguin Book of Women Poets,* edited by Carol Cosman, Joan Keefe, and Kathleen Weaver. Published by Penguin Books. Copyright © 1978 by Carol Cosman, Joan Keefe, and Kathleen Weaver.

"Night," by William Blake, from *William Blake: A Selection of Poems and Letters.* Edited with an introduction by Jacob Bronowski. Published by Penguin Books. Copyright © 1958 by J. Bronowski.

"Vespers," from *The Oxford Book of Prayer.* General editor, George Appleton. Oxford and New York: Oxford Univ. Press, 1988.

"Even at prayer, our eyes look inward," by Ghalib, translation copyright © 1989 by Jane Hirshfield. Used by permission of Jane Hirshfield.

"Evening Prayer," by Rabindranath Tagore, from *Gitanjali: A Collection of Indian Songs.* Published by Macmillan Publishing Co., 1971.

"Baruch Spinoza," from "Elegy," by Jorge Luis Borges, translated by Yirmiyahu Yovel. From *Spinoza and Other Heretics: The Marrano of Reason,* by Yirmiyahu Yovel. Copyright © 1989 by Princeton Univ. Press.

"I Can See in the Midst of Darkness," extracts from the writings of Mahatma Gandhi. From the compilation by M. K. Krishnan, Coimbatore, India. Navajivan Press.

"Afterwards," from *Collected Poems,* by Thomas Hardy. Copyright © 1925 by The Macmillan Company. Reprinted by permission of the Trustees of the Hardy Estate, The Macmillan Company of New York, Macmillan & Co. Ltd., London, and The Macmillan Company of Canada Ltd.

"A Hymn to the Night," by Novalis, translated by Dick Higgins. From *Hymns to the Night.* Revised edition. Translation copyright © 1978, 1984. McPherson & Company. 1984.

From *Thoughts in Solitude,* by Thomas Merton. Dell Publishing Co., Inc. 1956. Copyright © 1956, 1958 by the Abbey of Our Lady of Gethsemani.

"Nocturn," from *Selected Poems,* by Kathleen Raine. Reprinted by permission of the publisher, Lindisfarne Press, Hudson, NY 12534.

"Among the Sounds of the Night," from "Knoxville Summer of 1915," from *A Death in the Family,* by James Agee. Copyright © 1957 by The Agee Trust, copyright © renewed 1958 by Mia Agee. Reprinted by permission of Grosset & Dunlap, Inc.

"Thanks," from *The Rain in the Trees,* by W. S. Merwin. Copyright © 1988 by W. S. Merwin. Reprinted by permission of Alfred A. Knopf, Inc.

"Faith," from *Where Many Rivers Meet,* by David Whyte. Langley: Many Rivers Press, 1990. Copyright © 1990 by David Whyte. Reprinted by permission of the author.

"Listening," from *Stories That Could Be True: New and Collected Poems,* by William Stafford. Reprinted by permission of the estate of William Stafford.

"Summer Night," by Joy Harjo, from *In Mad Love & War.* Copyright © 1990 by Joy Harjo. Reprinted by permission of the University Press of New England.

"Night Game," by Rolfe Humphries. From *Collected Poems of Rolfe Humphries.* Reprinted by permission of Charles Scribner's Sons, 1948.

"Evening Ritual," from *Breakfast at the Victory,* by James P. Carse. HarperSanFrancisco, 1994.

"Knowing the Prayer," from *The Gates of the Forest,* by Elie Wiesel. Holt, Rinehart & Winston, 1966.

"Blue Mosque Reverie," by Phil Cousineau. Used by permission of the author.

"Night and Sleep," by Maulana Jalaluddin Rumi, from *Night and Sleep,* versions by Coleman Barks and Robert Bly. Published by Yellow Moon Press, 1981. Copyright © by Coleman Barks and Robert Bly.

To Sleep, Perchance, to Dream

"Let Sleep Not Come Upon Thy Languid Eyes" attributed to Pythagoras, and quotes by Epictetus and da Vinci, cited in *The Bed: or the Clinophile's Vade Mecum,* by Cecil and Margery Gray. London & Redhill: Love & Malcomson Ltd., 1946.

"Golden Slumber," by Thomas Dekker, cited in *The Oxford Dictionary of Quotations,* 3d ed., 1980.

"What an Excellent Thing Slumber Is," by Thomas Dekker, cited in *Lewis Carroll's Bedside Book,* edited by Edgar Cuthwellis. Published by Houghton Mifflin Company, 1979.

"Sonnet XXVII," by William Shakespeare. Various editions.

"The Sweet Sleep of Penelope and Odysseus," excerpt from *The Odyssey,* by Homer. Translated by A. T. Murray. Various editions.

Excerpt from "Sleep and Poetry," by John Keats. From *John Keats: The Complete Poems.* Edited by John Barnard. Third edition. Published by Penguin Books, 1988.

"The Way to Lie in Bed," by Robert Burton, from *The Anatomy of Melancholy;* excerpt from *The Last Days of Immanuel Kant,* by Thomas De Quincey; and "Going to Bed with Music," by Sir Thomas Browne, cited in *The Bed: or the Clinophile's Vade Mecum,* by Cecil and Margery Gray. London & Redhill: Love & Malcomson Ltd., 1946.

"A Medieval Remedy for Wasteful Sleeplessness," by Marsilio Ficino. Translated by Charles Boer. From *The Book of Life,* by Marsilio Ficino. Spring Publications, Inc., 1992. Copyright © 1980 by Charles Boer.

"Beethoven's Night Thoughts to His Immortal Beloved," from *A Treasure House of the World's Great Letters.* Edited by M. Lincoln Schuster. Copyright © 1940 and 1968 by Simon & Schuster, Inc.

"Bringing Sleep to Weary Bodies," by Erasmus, "At Night," by John Calvin, from *The Oxford Book of Prayer.* General editor, George Appleton. Oxford and New York: Oxford Univ. Press, 1988.

Excerpt from "The Parted Lovers," from *American Indian Poetry: An Anthology of Songs and Chants.* Edited by George W. Cronyn. New York: Ballantine Books, 1991. Copyright renewed © 1962 by George W. Cronyn.

"Night," by Eduardo Galeano, from *Memory of Fire: Genesis.* Translated by Cedric Belfrage. Translation copyright © 1985 by Cedric Belfrage. Reprinted by permission of Pantheon Books, a division of Random House, Inc.

"The Midnight Guest," from *Sappho and the Greek Lyric Poets* by Willis Barnstone, translator. Copyright © 1962, 1967, 1988 by Willis Barnstone. Reprinted by permission of Schocken Books, published by Pantheon Books, a division of Random House, Inc.

"Chuang Tzu's Dream," by Chuang Tzu, translated by Lin Yutang. Cited in *Parabola* 7, no. 1.

"A Dream of Mountaineering," by Po Chü-i, translated by Arthur Waley. Copyright © 1919, 1940 by Alfred A. Knopf, Inc.

"Dance of the Spirits," by Salvador Cuevas, from *The Way We Lived,* by Malcolm Margolin. Copublished by Heyday Books and the California Historical Society. Copyright © 1981 by Malcolm Margolin.

"I Fell Asleep," by Ono No Komachi. Translated by Kenneth Rexroth in *Love Poems from the Japanese.* Edited by Sam Hamill. Shambhala Publications, 1994.

"Echo," by Christina Rossetti, "The Vision to Electra," by Robert Herrick, "The Visionary," by Emily Brontë, and "Meeting at Night," by Robert Browning, various editions.

"Last Night I Had a Dream," reprinted by permission of the publishers from *Antonio Machado: Selected Poems,* translated by Alan S. Trueblood, Cambridge, Mass.: Harvard Univ. Press, Copyright © 1982 by the President and Fellows of Harvard College.

"Lethe," by Charles Baudelaire, from *Selected Poems of Charles Baudelaire.* Translated by Geoffrey Wagner. Used by permission of Grove/Atlantic, Inc.

"A Dream Within a Dream," from *A Collection of Poems by Edgar Allan Poe.* Grey Walls Press Ltd., 1948.

"Dreaming by the River," excerpt from *A Week on the Concord and Merrimack Rivers,* by Henry David Thoreau. Various editions. Originally published, 1849.

Excerpt from "The Sleepers," by Walt Whitman. From *The Complete Poems,* by Walt Whitman. Edited by Francis Murphy. Penguin Books Ltd., 1979.

"I'm Going to Sleep," by Alfonsina Storni, and "When with You Asleep," by Juan Ramón Jiménez. From *Love Poems from Spain and Spanish America.* English translations copyright © 1986 by Perry Higman. Reprinted by permission of City Lights Books.

"Falling Down Roads of Sleep," by Quincy Trope. From *Weather Reports: New & Selected Poems.* Harlem River Press. Copyright © 1991 by Quincy Troupe.

"Sleep, Darling," from *Sappho: A New Translation,* by Mary Barnard. Published by the Univ. of California Press. Copyright © 1958 by the Regents of the University of California; copyright © renewed 1984 by Mary Barnard.

"Sleep, Baby, Sleep," from *The Real Mother Goose.* Rand McNally & Co., 1916. Copyright © renewed 1944.

"The Land of Nod," by Robert Louis Stevenson. From *A Children's Garden of Verses.* Avenel Books by arrangement with Charles Scribner's Sons.

"Humming Home Your Shadow," retold from the Hoopa by Sister Maria José Hobday. Cited in *Parabola 7,* no. 1.

"Looking at Them Asleep," from *The Gold Cell,* by Sharon Olds. Copyright © 1987 by Sharon Olds. Reprinted by permission of Alfred A. Knopf, Inc.

"Hearing My Prayers," by Jeff Poniewaz. Published by permission of the author.

"In No Way," by David Ignatow, from *New & Collected Poems,* 1970–1985. Copyright © 1986 by David Ignatow, Wesleyan Univ. Press. Used by permission of the University Press of New England.

Poem XII of "Twenty-One Love Poems" is reprinted from *The Dream of a Common Language: Poems 1974–1977* by Adrienne Rich, by permission of the author and W. W. Norton & Company, Inc. Copyright © 1978 by W. W. Norton & Company, Inc.

"Sleeping Habit," by Yasunari Kawabata, from *Palm-Sized Stories.* Translated by Lane Dunlop and J. Martin Holman. North Point Press, 1988. Copyright © by Hite Kawabata. English translations copyright © 1988 by Lane Dunlop and J. Martin Holman.

"And Now You're Mine," from *100 Love Sonnets,* by Pablo Neruda. Translated by Stephen Tapscott. Univ. of Texas Press, 1986. Copyright © 1959 by Pablo Neruda and Fundación Pablo Neruda. Copyright © 1986 by the Univ. of Texas Press. Reprinted by permission of the Univ. of Texas Press.

"Wild Nights—Wild Nights!" by Emily Dickinson. Edited by Thomas H. Johnson. Published by Little, Brown & Company Ltd. Copyright © 1951, 1955 by the President and Fellows of Harvard College. Copyright © 1952 by Alfred Leete Hampson. Copyright © 1957, 1958, 1960 by Mary L. Hampson.

"Winged Man," by Glenn Ingersoll, was originally published in *Carolina Quarterly,* Fall 1993. It is reprinted by permission of the poet.

"Fall of the Evening Star," from *The Love Poems of Kenneth Patchen,* by Kenneth Patchen. City Lights Books, San Francisco, 1966.

"Sleeping on the Wing," from *Collected Poems* by Frank O'Hara. Copyright © 1971 by Maureen Granville-Smith, Administratrix of the Estate of Frank O'Hara. Reprinted by permission of Alfred A. Knopf, Inc.

Burning the Midnight Oil

"Night Rules," from *The Wisdom of the Desert: Sayings from the Desert Fathers of the Fourth Century.* Translated by Thomas Merton. Boston & London: Shambhala Publications, 1994.

"The Sentinel in Love," by Farid ud-Din Attar. Rendered into English by C. S. Nott from the French translation of Garcin de Tassy. From *The Conference of Birds.* Shambhala Publications, Inc., 1971. Copyright © 1954 by C. S. Nott.

"A Prayer to the Gods of Night," translated from Sumerian by N. K. Sandars. From *Poems of Heaven and Hell from Ancient Mesopotamia.* Penguin Books, 1971. Copyright © 1971 by N. K. Sandars.

"The Sleep Test," from *The Storytelling Stone.* Edited and with an introduction by Susan Feldman. Dell Publishing Co., Inc., 1965. Copyright © 1965 by Susan Feldman.

"Gethsemane," retold by Stephen Mitchell, from *The Gospel According to Jesus.* HarperCollins, 1992. Copyright © 1992 by Stephen Mitchell.

"Drinking Alone by Moonlight," by Li Po, translated by Arthur Waley. From *Translations from the Chinese.* Alfred A. Knopf, Inc. Copyright © 1919 and renewed 1947.

"A Medieval Jewish Prayer," by Nechum Bronze. From *The Oxford Book of Prayer.* General editor, George Appleton. Oxford and New York: Oxford Univ. Press, 1988.

"On the Beach at Night," from *The Complete Poems,* by Walt Whitman. Edited by Francis Murphy. Penguin Books Ltd., 1979.

"Each Breath of Night," excerpt from *Teaching a Stone to Talk,* by Annie Dillard. Harper Colophon, 1983. Copyright © 1982 by Annie Dillard.

"Acquainted with the Night," from *The Poetry of Robert Frost.* Edited by Edward Connery Lathem. Copyright © 1956 by Robert Frost. Copyright © 1928, 1969 by Henry Holt and Co., Inc. Reprinted by permission of Henry Holt and Co., Inc.

"The Heart of Herakles," by Kenneth Rexroth: From *The Collected Shorter Poems of Kenneth Rexroth.* Copyright © 1966 by Kenneth Rexroth. Reprinted by permission of New Directions Publishing Corp.

"Glaciers by Starlight," from *The Wilderness World of John Muir.* With an introduction and interpretive comments by Edwin Way Teale. Houghton Mifflin Co. Copyright © 1954 by Edwin Way Teale.

"Alone in the Arctic Night," by Richard E. Byrd, from *Alone.* Island Press, 1984. Copyright © 1938 by Richard E. Byrd. Copyright renewed 1966 by Marie A. Byrd.

"Night Flight," by Beryl Markham, from *West with the Night.* North Point Press, 1983. Copyright © 1942, 1983 by Beryl Markham.

"Rhyming in the Darkness," by Chet Raymo. Excerpt from *Honey from Stone: A Naturalist's Search for God* by Chet Raymo.

"El Greco's Parable of Genius," from *Eternal Moment: Selected Poems,* by Sándor Weöres. Copyright © 1988, New Rivers Press.

"Piano Man," from *Portal,* by Joyce Jenkins. Santa Fe: A Pennywhistle Chapbook, 1993. Copyright © 1993 by Joyce Jenkins. Reprinted by permission of the author.

"Childfoot Visitation" originally appeared in *Last Words* by Antler, Ballantine Books' Available Press, 1986. Copyright Antler.

"Runaway," by Kenneth Rexroth. From *The Collected Shorter Poems of Kenneth Rexroth.* Reprinted by permission of New Directions Publishing Corp. Copyright © 1966 by Kenneth Rexroth.

"Ballad of the Dogs," by Lars Gustafsson. From *The Stillness of the World Before Bach.* Copyright © 1988 by Lars Gustafsson. Reprinted by permission of New Directions Publishing Corp.

The Dark Night of the Soul

"Insomnia," by Abū 'Āmir ibn al-Hammārah. Translated by Cola Franzen in *Poems of Arab Andalusia.* English translation copyright © 1989 by Cola Franzen. Reprinted by permission of City Lights Books.

"All Night I Could Not Sleep," by Zi Ye, and "Winter Night," by Yang-ti, translated by Arthur Waley. Alfred A. Knopf, Inc. Copyright © 1919, 1940.

"Untouched by Sleep," by Ovid. Translated by Christopher Marlowe. Cited in *The Bed: or the Clinophile's Vade Mecum,* by Cecil and Margery Gray. London & Redhill: Love & Malcomson Ltd., 1946.

"Folk Rhyme," traditional English. Cited in *Death: An Anthology of Ancient Texts, Songs, Prayers, and Stories.* Edited by David Meltzer. North Point Press, 1984. Copyright © 1984 by David Meltzer.

"Night Rain," from *The Ink Dark Moon,* by Jane Hirshfield and Mariko Aratami. Copyright © 1990 by Jane Hirshfield. Reprinted by permission of Vintage Books, a division of Random House, Inc.

Reconciling with the Night

Excerpt from "Self-Reliance," from *The Best of Ralph Waldo Emerson.* Copyright © 1941 by Walter J. Black, Inc.

"Hold On in the Darkness," from "Auguries and Innocence," by William Blake. From *William Blake: A Selection of Poems and Letters.* Edited with an introduction by Jacob Bronowski. Penguin Books, 1958. Copyright © 1958 by J. Bronowski.

Excerpt from *Meditations,* by Marcus Aurelius. Translated with an introduction by Maxwell Staniforth. Penguin Books, 1964. Copyright © 1964 by Maxwell Staniforth.

"Once Calmed," by Lao Tzu. Excerpt from page 7 of *Hua Hu Ching: The Unknown Teachings of Lao Tzu,* by Brian Walker. Copyright © 1992 by Brian Browne Walker. Reprinted by permission of HarperCollins Publishers.

"Before Turning Off the Lights," from "Encounter with God Through the Senses," by Brother David Steindl-Rast. From *For the Love of God.* Edited by Benjamin Shields and Richard Carlson. HarperSanFrancisco, 1990.

"Where Is the Nightingale," by H. D. From *Selected Poems.* Copyright © 1982 by the Estate of Hilda Doolittle. Reprinted by permission of New Directions Publishing Corp.

"Lead, Kindly Light," by John Henry Newman.

"The Gentle Rapping," by Simon Pokagon. From *Native American Wisdom.* Running Press, 1993.

"Peace," by Walter de la Mare. Reprinted by permission of the Literary Trustees of Walter de la Mare and the Society of Authors as their representatives.

"Human Wisdom," by Charles Péguy. From *Short Prayers for the Long Day,* compiled by Giles and Melville Harcourt. Collins, 1978.

"The Starlight Night," by Gerard Manley Hopkins.

"Solitude," from *A Sport and a Pastime,* by James Salter. North Point Press, 1978. Copyright © 1978 by James Salter.

"In a Dark Time," from *The Far Field,* by Theodore Roethke. Copyright © 1964. Used by permission of Doubleday, a division of Bantam Doubleday Publishing Group, Inc.

"The Song of a Man Who Has Come Through," by D. H. Lawrence. From *The Complete Poems of D. H. Lawrence* by D. H. Lawrence. Edited by V. de Sola Pinto & F. W. Roberts. Copyright © 1964, 1971 by Angelo Ravagli and C. M. Weekley, Executors of the Estate of Frieda Lawrence Ravagli. Used by permission of Viking Penguin, a division of Penguin Books USA, Inc.

"Reconciliation," by Else Lasker-Schüler, from *Gesammelte Werke in Drei Bänden.* Band 1. *Gedichte 1902–1943.* Translated by Robert Alter. Munich: Kösel, 1961.

"The Vast Night," by Rainer Maria Rilke, translated by Stephen Mitchell.

"Dawn," by Juana Ibarbourou. From *Love Poems from Spain and Spanish America.* Selected and translated by Perry Higman. City Lights Publishing, 1986. Translations copyright © by Perry Higman.

"The Gift," by Maurya Simon, from *The Enchanted Room.* Copyright © 1986 by Maurya Simon. Reprinted by permission of Copper Canyon Press, P.O. Box 271 Port Townsend, WA 98368.

"The Night-Blooming Cereus," by Robert Hayden. Reprinted from *Collected Poems of Robert Hayden*. Edited by Frederick Glaysher, with the permission of Liveright Publishing Corporation. Copyright © 1972 by Robert Hayden.

"June Intercedes in the Garden of Roses," by Elizabeth Macklin. Copyright © 1994 by The New York Times Company. Reprinted by permission.

"Night Stock," from *Red-Haired Android*, by Jeremy Reed. Copyright © 1992 by Jeremy Reed. Reprinted by permission of City Lights Books.

"The Night View of the World," from *The Inward Journey*, by Howard Thurman. Copyright © 1961 Howard Thurman. Howard Thurman Educational Trust, 2020 Stockton Street, San Francisco, CA 94133.

"The Grandeur of a New Sunrise," by Pierre Teilhard de Chardin, translated by Simon Bartholomew. From *Hymn of the Universe*, by Pierre Teilhard de Chardin. Copyright © 1961 by Editions du Seuil. Copyright © 1965 in the English translation by William Collins Sons & Co Ltd., London, and Harper & Row, Inc., New York.

"The White Heart of God," from *The Great Fires, Poems, 1982–1992*, by Jack Gilbert. Reprinted by permission of Alfred A. Knopf, Inc. Copyright © 1994 by Jack Gilbert.

"The Still Time," by Galway Kinnell, from *Mortal Acts, Mortal Words*. Copyright © 1980 by Galway Kinnell. Reprinted by permission of Houghton Mifflin Co. All rights reserved.

"Before Dawn . . . ," by Tom Clark. Copyright © 1992 by Tom Clark. Reprinted from *Sleepwalker's Fate: New and Selected Poems 1965–1991* with permission of Black Sparrow Press.

"Phantasmagoria," from *Lewis Carroll's Bedside Book: Entertainment for the Wakeful Hours*. Edited by Edgar Cuthwellis. Published by Houghton Mifflin Company, 1979.

"Sleepwalking," from *Going to Bed*, by Anthony Burgess. New York: Abbeville Press Publishers, 1982. Copyright © 1982 by Anthony Burgess.

"Night Wood (Duo)," by Anna Wickham, from *The Writings of Anna Wickham*. Edited by R. D. Smith. Reprinted by kind permission of the publishers, Virago Press Ltd.

"The Peace of Wild Things," by Wendell Berry, from *Openings*. Reprinted by permission of Harcourt Brace Jovanovich, Inc., 1968. Copyright © 1968 by Wendell Berry.

"Demeter," by Genevieve Taggard, from *Slow Music*. Copyright © 1946 by Harper & Brothers, Publishers; copyright renewed. Reprinted by permission of Marcia D. Liles.

The Hush of Dawn

Excerpt from "Songs of Owl Woman," by Owl Woman (Juana Manwell), translated by Frances Densmore. From *Papago Music*, Bulletin 90 of the Bureau of American Ethnology. Published by the Smithsonian Institution. Copyright © 1929 by Frances Densmore.

"Wake!" Excerpt from "The Rubáiyát of Omar Khayyám," from the translation of Edward Fitzgerald. 5th edition.

"Dawn Prayer," by South African Bushman, from *The Oxford Book of Prayer*. General editor, George Appleton. Oxford and New York: Oxford Univ. Press, 1988.

"Night," by Federico García Lorca. From *The Selected Poems of Federico García Lorca.* Copyright © 1955 by New Directions Publishing Corp. Reprinted by permission of New Directions Publishing Corp.

"Lying Single in Bed," by Samuel Pepys. Cited in *The Bed: or the Clinophile's Vade Mecum,* by Cecil and Margery Gray. London & Redhill: Love & Malcomson Ltd., 1946.

"The Sweetest Night," by Mrs. Jonathan Edwards. Cited in *The Varieties of Religious Experience.* Mentor Books, 1958.

"Early Dawn," from *We Women,* by Edith Södergran. Translated by Samuel Charters.

"Hearing the Sun Singing," by Black Elk, with John Neihardt, from *Black Elk Speaks,* by John Neihardt. University of Oklahoma Press.

"The Advancing Dawn," by Ohiyesa, translated by T. C. McLuhan. From *Touch the Earth,* by T. C. McLuhan.

"To Tan Ch'iu," by Li Po, translated by Arthur Waley. From *Translations from the Chinese.* Alfred A. Knopf, Inc. Copyright © 1919 and renewed 1947.

"I Sought My Lover at Twilight." Excerpt from page 105 of *The Turquoise Bee: Love Poems of the Sixth Dalai Lama,* by Rick Fields, Mayumi Oda, and Brian Cutillo. Copyright © 1994 by Rick Fields, Brian Cutillo, and Mayumi Oda. Reprinted by permission of HarperCollins Publishers.

"A Riddling Tale," from *The Complete Grimm's Fairy Tales.* Translated by Margaret Hunt and revised by James Stern. Copyright © 1944 by Pantheon Books Inc. Copyright © renewed 1972 by Random House, Inc.

"Is This Darkness the Night of Power," by Bibi Hayati. Excerpt from page 169 of *Women in Praise of the Sacred.* Edited by Jane Hirshfield. Copyright © 1994 by Jane Hirshfield. Reprinted by permission of HarperCollins Publishers.

"The Night at Zenshō-ji Temple," by Matsuo Bashō, translated by Dorothy Britton. From *On a Narrow Road to a Far Province.* Revised edition. Kodansha International, 1980.

"The Horses," from *The Hawk in the Rain,* by Ted Hughes. Reprinted by permission of Faber and Faber Ltd.

"The Daled," from *Searching for the Ox,* by Louis Simpson. Copyright © 1976 by Louis Simpson. By permission of William Morrow & Inc.

"The Blind Watchmaker," by Phil Cousineau. Copyright © 1994 by Phil Cousineau. Used by permission of the author.

"In The Ashes of Night," by Noah benShea, from *Jacob the Baker.* Published by Ballantine Books. Copyright © 1989 by Noah benShea.

"The Poet," from the cycle "Secrets of the Craft" by Anna Akhmatova is reprinted with permission from *The Complete Poems of Anna Akhmatova,* second edition, Zephyr Press, 1992. Translated and copyright by Judith Hemschemeyer, 1990, 1992.

Excerpt from *The Tempest,* by William Shakespeare. Various editions.

"Greeting to Day," by Orpingalik, from *Eskimo Poems from Canada and Greenland.* Translated by Tom Lowenstein. Copyright © by Tom Lowenstein. Used by permission of the author.